Meaning and Modality

Meaning and Modality

CASIMIR LEWY

CAMBRIDGE UNIVERSITY PRESS

CAMBRIDGE

LONDON · NEW YORK · MELBOURNE

Published by the Syndics of the Cambridge University Press
The Pitt Building, Trumpington Street, Cambridge CB2 1RP
Bentley House, 200 Euston Road, London NW1 2DB
32 East 57th Street, New York, NY 10022, USA
296 Beaconsfield Parade, Middle Park, Melbourne 3206, Australia

First published 1976

Printed in Great Britain
at the
University Printing House, Cambridge
(Harry Myers, University Printer)

Library of Congress Cataloguing in Publication Data

Lewy, Casimir.

Meaning and modality.

Includes index.

1. Meaning (Philosophy) 2. Modality (Logic) 1. Title.

B105.M4L48   121   76-11084

ISBN 0 521 21314 2

TO E.L.

CONTENTS

PREFACE

As this book has been a very long time in the writing, I think I ought to describe in some detail its origin.

I first became interested in some of the problems with which this book is concerned in the academic year 1938–39 when as a third year undergraduate I attended G. E. Moore's lectures on "Metaphysics". John Wisdom's paper on "Metaphysics and Verification" had just been published in *Mind*, and Moore devoted the earlier portions of his course to a discussion of Wisdom's view that the three propositions:

(1) "Vixen" means the same as "female fox";

(2) "Vixen" means "female fox";

(3) A vixen may be defined as a female fox;

all "make the same factual claims".

I think I learned more from that course of lectures and from Moore's course in the preceding academic year than I learned from any other lectures that I ever attended. But his treatment of Wisdom's (1), (2) and (3) was exceedingly unsatisfactory. This was due to a variety of reasons, of which the main were perhaps the following.

He did not attempt to explain precisely the respective ways in which the three sentences in question were supposed to be used.

He used "entails" in a sense in which it obviously did not mean "strictly implies", but made no attempt to explain *how* he was using it. This did not matter much in many of Moore's other lectures: one could in general replace "entails" by "strictly implies" without affecting the validity of Moore's arguments. But it did matter very much indeed in connexion with his discussion of the relationship between (1) and (2) on the one hand, and (3) on the other hand. For in the earlier part of the course he maintained that (3) makes *no verbal claims*; and he clearly implied, although he did not expressly assert it, that he thought (3) to be logically necessary.

He also made no attempt to discuss the Paradox of Analysis: he merely said, first, that if (3) makes no verbal claims, then it seems to follow that (3) is identical with:

A female fox may be defined as a female fox;
and, secondly, that he did not think that this does really follow.

Finally, and most importantly, he suddenly announced that he had changed his mind and now thought that (3) *does* make some verbal claims. But he did not explain *why* he had changed his mind so radically or *what* verbal claims he now took (3) to be making.

As a result of all this, no clear or indeed coherent treatment of the subject emerged from the lectures.

Early in 1943 I myself began to lecture for the Faculty of Moral Science, and I decided to deal with Wisdom's three propositions in my own way. But for a very long time I could make no real progress, partly because I got entangled in the problem of the relationship between entailment and strict implication. For instance, I had acquired during my undergraduate years the belief – which seemed to be then common at Cambridge – that a contingent proposition cannot entail a necessary proposition; and it took me a long time to see that this was not so. And of course this in itself went only a very small way towards solving the problem.

In 1952 I returned to Cambridge after an absence of seven years; and in 1953–54 I gave a course of lectures dealing with the three propositions of Wisdom's as well as with the problem of entailment. This was a poor course, and I was very dissatisfied with it. I therefore revised it substantially for 1954–55.

This new version I repeated with only slight changes in 1955–56 and 1956–57. But then I became dissatisfied with the new version too, and I altered it considerably for 1957–58. The third substantial revision came in 1958–59, the fourth in 1963–64, the fifth in 1965–66 and the sixth in 1968–69. In 1970–71 I decided to alter the course again, and this time I made even more extensive changes and additions than on any other single occasion before. And I again revised the course for 1973–74.

The present book is based primarily on that last course; but it incorporates many alterations and also some earlier material which I did not discuss in that particular year. Finally, I have added a fair amount of material that is entirely new.

I fear that in spite of the length of time which it has taken me to produce it, the book may still contain many mistakes. And I am aware of the fact that the arrangement of it is far from ideal. But I am certain that if I tried to continue to revise and re-arrange it, I should *never* finish it.

There are a few other matters that I think I should mention.

The reader cannot fail to notice that I attack strongly certain views expressed by Professor John Wisdom. In all probability, he no longer holds those views himself; and in any case, I am concerned *solely* with the question of their truth or falsity. In fact, my debt to Wisdom is very considerable for he was my supervisor when I was an undergraduate, and I remember with deep gratitude the *immense* amount of trouble which he took in teaching me. I do not think that our weekly supervision, which was supposed to last one hour, *ever* lasted less than two!

I have not had the good fortune to study under Professor Quine. But although on many matters I sharply disagree with him, I am very conscious of the fact that I have learned a great deal from his published writings.

I do not attach much importance to questions of priority, and I have not therefore troubled to indicate when I first included the material contained in this book in my lectures.[1] The only partial exception which I have allowed myself to make occurs in the portions of the book concerning entailment. This is due partly to the fact that in the many years since I started thinking about it, my views on entailment have undergone radical changes. And partly because a good deal of literature, some of it highly technical, has appeared on the subject in the last few years. Owing to the pressure of other duties, I have not been able to read more than a small proportion of that literature; and I think it is possible that some of the ideas at which I have arrived so laboriously, and have probably expressed rather badly, have been arrived at independently by others, and have been expressed by them in a much better way. If this is so, I should be pleased, but I thought it legitimate to mention when I myself first stated them in lectures.

Trinity College,   C. LEWY
Cambridge
November 1975

---

[1] Wittgenstein once said to me that "to publish" means "to make public", and that therefore lecturing is a form of publication. He was, of course, entirely right. But this meaning of the word appears to be obsolete in present-day academic English.

I

Words and concepts

In "Metaphysics and Verification" Wisdom says:

> To say that analytic statements are verbal is useful if one wishes
> to get rid of the idea that they differ from statements about
> words in the way that statements about dogs differ from state-
> ments about cats or statements about colour differ from state-
> ments about shape and size. One might express this by saying
> that to say that analytic propositions are verbal is useful in
> getting rid of the idea that they differ from ones that are not
> analytic in being about a new species of thing or 'in subject-
> matter'. I shall use the last expression although it involves
> deciding arbitrarily not to describe the sort of difference there is
> between analytic and verbal statements as a difference in subject-
> matter. The excuse for doing this is that for every statement
> about abstract entities – propositions, characteristics – there is a
> verbal statement which makes the same factual claims though its
> meaning is different. I have explained this point elsewhere,[1] but
> it is of such importance that I must explain it briefly here.
>
> If I say 'good' means 'approved by the majority', in so far
> as I make any factual claims they are justified by what people
> would say, that is, are verbal; but my purpose, or primary
> intention, in saying so, is not verbal. Suppose a Chinaman is
> decoding an English message, and does not know the meaning
> either of 'vixen' or of 'female fox', but says after investigation,
> '"vixen" means the same as "female fox"'. He says this though
> he knows his hearer also does not know the meaning of either
> expression. Suppose now Smith says '"vixen" means "female
> fox"', because he believes his hearer knows the meaning of 'female
> fox' but not of 'vixen'. Suppose now someone says, 'A vixen
> may be defined as a female fox'. The factual claims involved in

---

[1] Here Wisdom refers to his paper in *Psyche*, vol. 13, pp. 166–9, and his paper in
Mind, vol. 42, pp. 195–6. We shall consider these references presently.

the statements are the same. But the purposes they serve are very different, and this makes us speak differently about their meanings. A hearer understands the Chinaman's statement though he understands neither 'vixen' nor 'female fox'; but only if he understands one of the two does he understand Smith, and only if he understands the meaning of both does he understand or, if you like, fully understand the philosop' er. Hence statements about propositions and characteristics such as 'He asserted the proposition that Africa is hot', 'She is chic', can be turned into statements about words 'He uttered the sentence "Africa is hot"', 'She is what the French call "chic"', if, and only if the verbal statements are so used that we say that a man understands them only if he understands not merely the expressions 'the sentence "Africa is hot"' and 'what the French call "chic"' but also understands the sentence 'Africa is hot' and the word 'chic'.[1]

There then follows the following footnote:

> (*a*) To deny this results in the extreme paradox '*All* statements are verbal'. (*b*) This is part of the explanation of the necessity of necessary statements. For such statements connect abstract things and are therefore purely verbal in a way in which 'He asserted Africa is hot' is not; that is, they are purely about the use of the expressions they connect. And what they assert must be known to the hearer if he understands them. Hence, if he denies them, the speaker says the hearer does not understand. This is characteristic of necessary statements. Logically necessary statements are checked by the actual usage of language and to this extent may be called true and false. Metaphysically necessary statements only have *excuses* in the actual use of language and so can only be called 'excusable' and 'inexcusable'.

There is no doubt about the importance of Wisdom's claims. If he is right, then (1) he has solved one of the principal problems in the philosophy of logic – the problem of the relation of propositions about abstract entities to propositions about words, and (2) he has gone at least some way to solve another of the principal problems in this field – the problem of the relation of logically necessary propositions to propositions about words. That is to say,

[1] J. Wisdom, "Metaphysics and Verification", *Mind*, vol. 47 (1938), p. 463. Reprinted, with slight changes, in J. Wisdom, *Philosophy and Psycho-analysis* (Oxford, 1953), pp. 62–3. I quote from the version as published in the book.

if he is right then he has explained the notion of an abstract entity, and has also gone some way towards explaining the notion of logical necessity.

It follows that by discussing Wisdom's claims we shall be considering one of the central areas in the philosophy of logic.

Let me now quote the two passages from his other writings to which Wisdom refers, and in which, he says, he has already "explained this point".

The essential parts of the first, from "Ostentation", read as follows:

> *The philosopher's statement is verbal.* All philosophic statements are, of course, made *in* words. We may go further, however; for all philosophic statements *mention* words.[1]

> It is not the primary intention of the philosopher to convey a fact about words; this is not because it is his primary intention to convey a fact which is not about words, but because it is not his primary intention to convey a fact at all. His primary intention is not to provide information but to promote insight... Thus the philosopher does not differ from the translator in *what* he says but in the *intention* with which he says it.[2]

The passage from "Logical Constructions" is very similar. I will only quote a part of it:

> I do not mean...that the philosopher is a translator. What the philosopher *says* is that one sentence can be substituted for another, but what he *does* is much more than this.[3]

As a matter of fact Wisdom refers to the problem in a fourth paper as well – viz. in "Philosophical Perplexity".[4] But this does not bring out anything essentially new, and I shall not quote from it now, though I will refer to it later.

I shall concentrate mainly on the long passage from "Metaphysics and Verification" – the latest of Wisdom's four discussions.

Let us then consider the following three propositions:

  (1) "Vixen" means the same as "female fox";

[1] *Psyche*, vol. 13 (1933), p. 166. Reprinted in *Philosophy and Psycho-analysis*, p. 3.
[2] P. 162 in *Psyche*; pp. 6–7 in *Philosophy and Psycho-analysis*.
[3] *Mind*, vol. 42 (1933), p. 195.
[4] *Proc. Aristotelian Soc.*, vol. 37 (1936–7). Reprinted in *Philosophy and Psycho-analysis* (see esp. pp. 38–9). I quote in the following pages from the reprinted article in the book.

(2) "Vixen" means "female fox";

(3) A vixen may be defined as a female fox.

It is of the utmost importance to realize that Wisdom is concerned with *a particular use* of each of these three sentences, and the first thing we must do is to explain the relevant use of each of them more fully than Wisdom does himself. In fact, Wisdom could have given just *one* sentence and distinguished three different uses of it.[1] We cannot therefore tell what propositions his sentences express just by looking at the sentences.

With this Wisdom would have agreed; but unfortunately his explanations are incomplete. He tells us that in order to understand sentence (1) it is not necessary to understand either the word "vixen" or the expression "female fox"; that in order to understand sentence (2) it is necessary to understand the expression "female fox"; and that in order to understand sentence (3) it is necessary to understand *both* the word "vixen" *and* the expression "female fox".[2]

Let us try to complete these explanations and thus specify the three propositions with which Wisdom is concerned.

I will do so as follows. I will in each case give a set of conditions which are severally necessary and jointly sufficient for saying that a man understands the sentence in question as Wisdom uses it.

(1) "Vixen" means the same as "female fox".

Explanation of Wisdom's use of (1)

X understands sentence (1) in the use with which Wisdom is concerned if and only if

(A) *X* understands the expression ""vixen"";[3]

(B) *X* understands the expression ""female fox"";

(C) *X* understands the expression "means the same as";

(D) *X* understands the syntax of (1).

---

[1] In fact, in "Philosophical Perplexity" he does give just one sentence, viz. '"Monarchy" means the same as "set of persons ruled by the same king"', and supposes that the decoder, the translator and the philosopher all use that one sentence.

[2] He actually says that in order to understand (2) it is necessary to understand *either* "vixen" *or* "female fox". I will assume, however, that he meant that it is necessary to understand "female fox" – to consider also the sentence ""Female fox" means vixen" would be merely tedious. He also talks about "understanding, or, if you like, fully understanding" sentence (3). I will disregard "fully understanding" – which is of no importance and would needlessly complicate the discussion.

[3] Except in actual quotations from other writers, I shall use only double quotes throughout this work. E.g. I shall write:

the expression ""vixen"",

not:

the expression "'vixen'".

I am using the word "syntax" here in a purely grammatical sense; and by "understanding the syntax of a sentence" I mean roughly understanding that which is conveyed by the order of the constituents of the sentence.

It should of course be noticed that (A) requires only that *X* should understand the expression ""vixen"" – *not* that *X* should understand the word "vixen"; and that (B) requires only that *X* should understand the expression ""female fox"" – *not* that he should understand the expression "female fox".

It is therefore clear that my conditions (A)–(D) do not contradict anything that Wisdom says in "Metaphysics and Verification", although they do contradict something that he says in "Philosophical Perplexity" (p. 38). For he says there that sentences such as (1) – "decoder's sentences" – can be understood by anybody who understands the meaning of "means the same as"! But this must have been due to carelessness or confusion.

For take condition (A). Surely, in order to understand (1) a man must know that the expression ""vixen"" is a name of the word "vixen"; and this is not entailed by condition (C), i.e. by the fact that he understands "means the same as". What *is* entailed by condition (C) is that the man in question knows that the expression ""vixen"" is a name of *some* word; but *not* that it is a name of the word "vixen". The same applies, *mutatis mutandis*, to the relation between (C) and (B). In fact I think it is clear that conditions (A), (B) and (C) form an independent set.[1] I also think that the conjunction of (A), (B) and (C) does not entail (D). But I will not discuss whether this is so: if I am wrong, then (D) is redundant, and this is not important for my purpose.

(2)   "Vixen" means female fox.

Explanation of Wisdom's use of (2)

X understands sentence (2) in the use with which Wisdom is concerned if and only if

      (A′)   *X* understands the expression ""vixen"";
      (B′)   *X* understands the expression "female fox";
      (C′)   *X* understands the word "means";
      (D′)   *X* understands the syntax of (2).

It should be noticed that (B′) – which does require that *X* should

---

[1] That is, the conjunction of (A) and (B) does not entail (C); the conjunction of (A) and (C) does not entail (B); and the conjunction of (B) and (C) does not entail (A).

understand the expression "female fox" – is the only condition which Wisdom gives; hence my explanation is consistent with his explanation. If there is another explanation of his use of (2) which is also consistent with his, but not equivalent to mine, then he has not explained his use of (2) unambiguously. (But I shall try to show later that no such alternative explanation would be coherent.)

As (2) can't be understood unless the expression "female fox" is understood, I think it is better to formulate (2) without putting "female fox" in quotes. This, which I have done above, does *not* prejudice the case against Wisdom. As I have already pointed out, he could have given just one sentence and distinguished three different uses of it. In any case, if anyone prefers to leave in the quotes he can do so, and my arguments won't be affected thereby.

What does Wisdom mean by saying that sentences (1), (2) and (3) "make the same factual claims"? It is surely odd that he nowhere explains it. From the quotations I have given it is however reasonably clear that at least one interpretation is as follows. When Wisdom says that (1), (2) and (3) make the same factual claims although their purpose is different, he is saying that the propositions expressed by (1), (2) and (3) are the same, but the point of asserting them is not the same. At any rate, that what the decoder, the transator and the philosopher *say* is the same, is what Wisdom is explicitly asserting both in "Ostentation" and in "Logical Constructions" – as my quotations show. And in "Philosophical Perplexity" – a later paper – he again says that the decoder, the translator and the philosopher "all use the same form of words because what they say is the same" (p. 38).

He does not say this explicitly in "Metaphysics and Verification"; but in view of the fact that he refers there to the two earlier papers in which, he says, he has already "explained the point", it seems reasonable to suppose that by saying that (1), (2) and (3) make the same factual claims, he meant that they all *say* the same – that they express the same proposition. In this case, the second part of his rather odd sentence "But the purposes they serve are very different, and this makes us speak differently about their meanings" must be interpreted to mean "and this tempts us to say that their meanings are different"; although if we did yield to this temptation we should be wrong.

Let us suppose, however, that in the last paper he has altered his position, and that by saying that sentences (1), (2) and (3) make the same factual claims he does *not* mean that they all express the same proposition. What, then, does he mean? I shall offer a weaker interpretation: I shall interpret him to mean that the propositions expressed by the three sentences are logically equivalent – that they all entail each other. (In 1942, at least, when I discussed this with him, Wisdom accepted this interpretation.)

Moreover, let us for the time being leave out (3) and consider (1) and (2) only. (We shall return to (3) later.)

My interpretation of Wisdom's assertion that (1) and (2) "make the same factual claims" is therefore that the proposition expressed by (1) entails and is entailed by the proposition expressed by (2). More fully:

(1) and (2) make the same factual claims if and only if (2) makes no factual claims which (1) doesn't make, *and* (1) makes no factual claims which (2) doesn't make.

This in turn means:

(2) makes no factual claims which (1) doesn't make if and only if the proposition expressed by (1) entails the proposition expressed by (2); (1) makes no factual claims which (2) doesn't make if and only if the proposition expressed by (2) entails the proposition expressed by (1).

At this stage, and until further notice, we shall always take "entails" to mean strictly implies ($\dashv$). That is to say, we shall take "P entails Q" to mean $\sim \Diamond (P \& \sim Q)$.[1] And I shall in fact, until further notice, use the symbol "$\dashv$" for "entails". Similarly, by "logical equivalence" or "mutual entailment" I shall, until further notice, mean strict equivalence, i.e. mutual strict implication, and I shall symbolize it by "$\equiv$".

So our questions are:

(A)   Does (1) $\dashv$ (2)?
(B)   Does (2) $\dashv$ (1)?

(It will have been noticed that I sometimes use numerals as labels for sentences and sometimes as labels for propositions. I believe that this ambiguity is always resolved by the context; but when it is especially important to avoid ambiguity, I use, e.g., the

---

[1] I.e. It is logically impossible that P be true and Q not true. (I use "$\sim$" for negation and "$\Diamond$" for logical possibility.) I believe that Wisdom meant by "entails" something narrower than "strictly implies". But his views on entailment are not clear, and I will discuss them later. It is obvious, however, that if one can show that P does *not* strictly imply Q, then *a fortiori* one will have shown that P does not *entail* Q.

phrase "sentence (1)" or the phrase "proposition (1)", as the case requires.) Let us first take (A).

I claim that (1) does *not* entail (2), and I have the following arguments for this.[1]

First argument. Let us translate sentences (1) and (2) into Latin. The translation of (1) is:

(1a) "Vixen" significat idem quam "female fox".

The translation of (2) is:

(2a) "Vixen" significat vulpem feminam.

It is clear that no Roman Cardinal could deduce (2a) from (1a) without Divine help.

The argument, fully stated, is as follows.[2]

(α) The Latin sentence (1a) is an exact translation of the English sentence (1), and the Latin sentence (2a) is an exact translation of the English sentence (2).

Hence:

(β) The proposition expressed by (1) is identical with the proposition expressed by (1a), and the proposition expressed by (2) is identical with the proposition expressed by (2a).

(γ) The proposition expressed by (1a) does not entail the proposition expressed by (2a).

(δ) If *P* is the same proposition as *Q*, then whatever is entailed by *P* is entailed by *Q* and vice versa.

From (β), (γ) and (δ) it follows:

(ε) The proposition expressed by (1) does not entail the proposition expressed by (2).

We can now add, for the sake of completeness,

(ζ) The proposition expressed by (1) is the proposition that

---

[1] The first two arguments are due essentially to Moore, although I state and develop them in my own way.

[2] This *type* of argument, often called the "translation argument", has been used by Church, Martha Kneale, Strawson, myself and others. It is credited by Church to a review by C. H. Langford (Langford, *Journal of Symbolic Logic*, vol. 2, no. 1, June 1937, p. 53). I believe Langford's review contained the first statement of it to appear in print. But it was used in lectures at Cambridge by G. E. Moore already in 1933–34. Cf. Moore's *Lectures on Philosophy* (London, 1966), p. 157. So far as its use by the other writers just mentioned is concerned, see C. Lewy, "Truth and Significance", *Analysis*, vol. 8 (1947); P. F. Strawson, "Truth", *Analysis*, vol. 9 (1949); A. Church, "On Carnap's Analysis of Statements of Assertion and Belief", *Analysis*, vol. 10 (1950); W. and M. Kneale, *The Development of Logic* (Oxford, 1962), pp. 50–1.

I will say more about the translation argument later (see Chapter 5).

It should also be noticed that I never rely on the translation argument alone.

"vixen" means the same as "female fox", and the proposition expressed by (2) is the proposition that "vixen" means female fox.

It follows immediately, from (ϵ) and (ζ), that (1) does not entail (2). Q.E.D.

This argument is absolutely conclusive, however fashionable it may be to hold otherwise. Those who think it is wrong should tell us exactly *what* is wrong with it. The mere dogmatic assertion that it *is* wrong simply won't do. And I have made it easier for them to do so by stating the argument fully.

But what *can* be wrong with it? One might perhaps claim that there are two senses of "expressing the same proposition" such that in one of them "(α) entails (β)" is true but (δ) is false, and in the other of which (δ) is true but "(α) entails (β)" is false. But I see no way in which this could be supported; and I think we can safely dismiss it. By manufacturing a non-existent ambiguity one could *pretend* to destroy *any* argument. I will leave it at this.

Second argument. As a matter of fact, however, there is no need for me to rely on the above argument, conclusive though it is. For there is a more direct argument which is also conclusive.

Is it logically impossible that (1) be true and (2) false? Clearly not: it is logically possible that the word "vixen" and the expression "female fox" should have meant the same, but that they should have meant white horse. In other words, (1) only tells us that "vixen" and "female fox" have *some* meaning in common; (1) entails nothing about *what* meaning they have in common. For this reason the clearest way of expressing (1) would be by saying ""vixen" means what is meant by "female fox"". On the other hand, (2) does tell us what the word "vixen" means; i.e. (2) does make a "factual claim" which (1) does not make. Hence, (1) does not entail (2).

A possible objection. Although this argument is quite conclusive, the following objection might be made to it. It might be said that if (1) is true, then anybody who uttered sentence (2) would by doing so express a true proposition in English. In other words, it might be claimed that (1) entails:

(2′)   ""Vixen" means female fox" expresses a true proposition in English.[1]

Two things should be said in reply to this. First, (1) does *not*

[1] I.e. ""Vixen" means female fox", as a sentence of English, expresses a true proposition.

entail (2′). For (2′) says something about the English word "means", and (1) does not. Secondly, (2′) does *not* entail (2): for if both "vixen" and "female fox" meant white horse, (2′) might have been true and yet (2) would have been false. Hence, even if (1) did entail (2′), this would provide no argument for supposing that (1) entails (2). (It should also be noticed that (2) does not entail (2′); but this I will discuss later.)

In brief, the objection confuses (2) with (2′), and is also mistaken in supposing that (1) entails (2′).

We can also see quite easily that (1) does not entail (2′) by translating both into another language, say Polish:

(1P) "Vixen" znaczy to samo co "female fox".

(2′P) ""Vixen" means female fox" wyraża prawdziwe zdanie w języku angielskim.

It is quite obvious that (1P) does not entail (2′P).

Third argument. Consider:

(α) In Polish "lisica" means the same as "lis płci żeńskiej".

I am assuming, of course, that in order to understand sentence (α) it is not necessary to know any Polish. In this respect (α) is like Wisdom's (1), although of course (α) and (1) express entirely different propositions. Now it seems to me obvious that (α) does not entail any proposition of the form of Wisdom's (2). For what would such a proposition be?

Suppose we say the proposition in question is:

(β) In Polish "lisica" means lis płci żeńskiej.

But this is not a well-formed sentence of English: it is meaningless unless it is taken to mean the same as (α), that is, unless it is interpreted to have quotes round "lis płci żeńskiej".

But clearly if (α) does not entail any proposition of the form of Wisdom's (2), how can (1) entail (2)? It cannot do so.

Another possible objection. Let us now consider the following three propositions:

(1) "Vixen" means the same as "female fox";

(1′) "Female fox" means female fox;

(2) "Vixen" means female fox.

It is of course understood that sentence (1) is elliptical for ""Vixen" *as a word of English* means the same as "female fox" *as an expression of English*"; that sentence (1′) is elliptical for ""Female fox" *as an expression of English* means female fox"; and that sentence (2) is elliptical for ""Vixen" *as a word of English* means female fox".

(That Wisdom's (1) and (2) must be taken to involve reference to English is obvious from the passage that I have quoted from "Metaphysics and Verification". And (1′) must of course be interpreted in the same way.)

Now there arises the following question. Does the *conjunction* of (1) and (1′) entail (2)? It does if we make the assumption that there is one and only one thing that "vixen" means, and one and only one thing that "female fox" means. Let us make this assumption (although in fact "vixen" in English has more than one meaning); and let us now consider the following objection. If the conjunction of (1) and (1′) entails (2), we imagine the objector to say, then since you are using "entails" to mean strictly implies, you will get immediately that (1) entails (2): for (1′) is logically necessary, and a logically necessary premiss can always be omitted.

Now we shall discuss this modal principle – that a necessary premiss can always be omitted – in greater detail later on. But the principle is certainly true. From:

$$(P \,\&\, Q) \dashv R$$

and

$$\sim \Diamond \sim Q$$

we can certainly deduce:

$$P \dashv R.$$

Hence, if (1′) were logically necessary, we should be able to conclude that, after all, (1) does entail (2).

But (1′) is *not* logically necessary. This is absolutely certain, and those who deny it are demonstrably confused. They include A. R. White,[1] and B. H. Medlin and J. J. C. Smart.[2] In fact it is certain that (1′) is contingent, for the following reasons.

(*a*)   Translate sentence (1′) into Latin, say. The result, ""Female fox" significat vulpem feminam", expresses a contingent proposition.

(*b*)   (1′) entails that "female fox" has *some* meaning in English – this is clearly contingent: "female fox" might not have meant anything in English. But a necessary proposition cannot entail a contingent one.

(*c*)   It is logically possible that "female fox" should have meant white horse.

[1] A. R. White, *G. E. Moore: A Critical Exposition* (Oxford, 1957), pp. 102–6.
[2] B. H. Medlin and J. J. C. Smart, "Moore's Paradox", *Analysis*, vol. 17 (1957).

We shall see later the multitude of false consequences that would follow if we supposed such propositions as $(1')$ to be necessary.

Strawson[1] takes as one of his examples:

> (S) "The monarch is deceased" means in English that the monarch is deceased.

He concedes all the arguments for the contingency of this (i.e. the arguments parallel to (a), (b) and (c) above), but says that although they are decisive against calling (S) necessary, they are very inadequate grounds for calling it, without qualification, "true and contingent".

Well, at least Strawson agrees that propositions such as $(1')$ are not logically necessary, which is all that we need for our purpose. But in fact, he should have gone further and agreed that they are contingent.

What must have been at the back of Strawson's mind is that you can't tell a man who doesn't understand the expression "female fox" what the expression means by using sentence $(1')$. This is true but irrelevant to the question of $(1')$'s necessity or contingency.

Of course, if we state the meaning of the English word "means", and assume that sentence $(1')$ is in accordance with the syntax of English, that ""female fox"" is a name of "female fox" and that "female fox" has *some* meaning in English, then it will follow that the *sentence* $(1')$, as a sentence of English, always expresses a true proposition. But from this it does *not* follow, and it is *not* true, that the *proposition* $(1')$ is logically necessary. A proposition is logically necessary if and only if its negation is logically impossible; and the negation of $(1')$ is not logically impossible. We must therefore distinguish between saying that a proposition is necessary and that a sentence always expresses a true proposition. From the latter the former does not follow. And notice in particular that although we can deduce that the *sentence* $(1')$ expresses a true proposition from premises which are solely about the English language, it does *not* follow from these premises that the *proposition* $(1')$ is logically necessary.

Also, a proposition is contingent if and only if neither it nor its negation is logically impossible. This is precisely the position with respect to $(1')$, and also with respect to Strawson's (S). A sentence such as $(1')$ may therefore perfectly well express a contingent proposition, even if one can't by using the sentence teach a man who doesn't understand "female fox" the meaning of this expression. We simply *must not* confuse these things.

Let us now consider question (B), i.e. the question whether Wisdom's (2) entails his (1).

The answer must again be in the negative, for the following reasons.

(*a*) *Translation argument.* Translate the two sentences into Latin, as before:

(1a) "Vixen" significat idem quam "female fox";

(2a) "Vixen" significat vulpem feminam.

It is quite clear that (2a) does not entail (1a).

(*b*) *Direct argument.* (1) entails that the expression "female fox" has *some* meaning in English; (2) does not entail this. But clearly if *P* entails *Q*, and *R* does not entail *Q*, then *R* does not entail *P*. Hence, (2) does not entail (1). In other words, (1) makes a "factual claim" which (2) does not make, viz. that "female fox" has *some* meaning in English, and hence (2) does not entail (1).

(*c*) Consider:

(*β*) "Lisica" in Polish means female fox;

(*α*) "Lisica" in Polish means the same as "lis płci żeńskiej".

(*α*) and (*β*) are of course entirely different propositions from (1) and (2); but it is obvious that (*β*) does not entail (*α*); and it should also be obvious that if (*β*) does not entail (*α*), then (2) does not entail (1).

A possible objection to the direct argument. The following objection may be made to this argument. If the expression "female fox" had no meaning, sentence (2) itself would have no meaning; hence, it may be said, proposition (2) does entail that "female fox" has meaning. The objection is mistaken; but I wish to consider it in detail because by doing so we shall be able to bring out certain points of considerable importance.

Consider the following propositions:

(2) "Vixen" means female fox;

(2*α*) The proposition expressed by the sentence ""Vixen" means female fox" is true;

(2*β*) The sentence ""Vixen" means female fox" expresses a proposition;

(2*γ*) The expression "female fox" has meaning.

What are the logical relations between these propositions?

Clearly:

(II)　$(2\alpha) \prec (2\beta)$;

(III)　$(2\beta) \prec (2\gamma)$;

hence

(IV)　$(2\alpha) \prec (2\gamma)$.

But the objection we are considering is that (2) entails (2γ), *not* that (2α) entails (2γ). Hence, the objector requires the extra premiss:

(I)　$(2) \prec (2\alpha)$.

And my claim is that *this* premiss is false: (2) does *not* entail (2α).

Those who think that (I) is true confuse (2α) with the following proposition:

$(2\alpha')$　The proposition that "vixen" means female fox is true.

But whilst (2) entails $(2\alpha')$, and $(2\alpha')$ entails (2), $(2\alpha')$ does *not* entail (2α), and (2α) does *not* entail $(2\alpha')$.

More generally, we must distinguish between:

(A)　The proposition that . . . is true (i.e. "It is true that . . .");

and

(B)　The proposition expressed by the sentence " . . . " is true.[1]

Propositions of the form (A) do not entail, and are not entailed by, the corresponding propositions of the form (B).[2]

The objection we are discussing confuses propositions of the form (A) with propositions of the form (B). (2α) is a proposition of the form (B) and it entails that the expression "female fox" has meaning: $(2\alpha')$ is a proposition of the form (A) and it does not entail this; and Wisdom's (2) is logically equivalent to $(2\alpha')$ and neither entails nor is entailed by (2α).

[1] This point is due essentially to Moore.

[2] Unless, of course, " . . . " expresses a necessary proposition, in which case a proposition of the form (A) will be trivially entailed by the corresponding proposition of the form (B). (It should be remembered that for the present I use "entails" to mean " $\prec$ ".) But this does not affect the argument given above.

2

Propositions and truth

In the last Chapter I distinguished between propositions of the form:

    (A)   The proposition that. . .is true,

and propositions of the form:

    (B)   The proposition expressed by the sentence ". . ." is true.

And I pointed out that propositions of the form (A) do not entail, and are not entailed by, the corresponding propositions of the form (B).[1]

Now it has often been said that truth presupposes meaningfulness; and we can now explain the sense in which this is true and the sense in which this is false. It is true if it means that propositions of the form (B) entail the corresponding propositions of the form:

    (C)   The sentence ". . ." is meaningful (i.e. expresses a proposition).

It is false if it means that propositions of the form (A) entail the corresponding propositions of the form (C).

It has also been said, e.g. by F. P. Ramsey, that the notion of truth is redundant (or otiose) on the ground that "*p* is true" means the same as "*p*".[2]

We can now also explain the sense in which *this* is true and the sense in which it is false. It is true if it means that propositions of the form (A) are logically equivalent to propositions of the form:

    (D)   . . .,

where the same sentence is substituted for ". . ." in (D) as in (A).

But Ramsey's assertion is false if it means that propositions of the form (B) are logically equivalent to the corresponding propositions of the form (D).

The distinction between propositions of the form of (A) and

---

[1] But see the preceding footnote.

[2] F. P. Ramsey, "Facts and Propositions", *Aristotlelian Soc. Suppl. Vol.* 7 (1927). Reprinted in F. P. Ramsey, *The Foundations of Mathematics and Other Logical Essays* (London, 1931), pp. 142–3.

propositions of the form of (B) is quite fundamental, and its disregard has led to serious errors.

I shall now discuss some of the implications of this distinction. By doing this we shall in fact be discussing a number of problems which are important in themselves.

In his *Introduction to Semantics* Carnap says:

> A remark may be added as to the way the term '*true*' is used in these discussions...We use the term here in such a sense that *to assert that a sentence is true means the same as to assert the sentence itself*; e.g. the two statements "The sentence 'The moon is round' is true" and "The moon is round" are merely two different formulations of the same assertion.[1]

A little lower down on the same page Carnap says that this is not, of course, a definition of the term "true", but rather a standard by which we judge whether a definition of truth is adequate, i.e. in accordance with our intention. And he goes on to say that if a definition of a predicate pr_i is proposed as a definition of truth, we shall accept it as an adequate definition if and only if on the basis of this definition pr_i fulfils the condition mentioned above, namely that it yields sentences like ""The moon is round" is...if and only if the moon is round", where pr_i (e.g. "true") is to be put in the place of "...".[2]

It is therefore clear that Carnap interprets the "if and only if" of Tarski's adequacy condition to mean at least "strictly implies and is strictly implied by". In fact he interprets it more strongly still to mean that the propositions:

The sentence "The moon is round" is true

and:

The moon is round

are identical. But I will disregard this and take him to be adopting the weaker interpretation given above.[3]

The very same interpretation was implicitly adopted by Quine in his review in the *Journal of Symbolic Logic* of an article by E. J. Nelson.[4] Quine here says:

[1] R. Carnap, *Introduction to Semantics* (Cambridge, Mass., 1942), p. 26.
[2] I shall call this condition "Tarski's adequacy condition for a definition of truth", or, for short, "Tarski's adequacy condition".
[3] We shall discuss later the *Tractatus*–Carnap view that strict equivalence is a sufficient (as well as a necessary) condition for propositional identity.
[4] W. V. O. Quine, Review of E. J. Nelson, "Contradiction and the Presupposition of Existence", *Journal of Symbolic Logic*, vol. 12 (1947), p. 55.

At the beginning of the discussion I showed that there is no need to allow inference of '*a* exists' from '*fa*' and from ' ∼ *fa*'. Now there is a curious line of thought, tangent at that point, which merits passing mention in conclusion. Viz.: Even if '*a* exists' cannot be inferred from '*fa*' and from ' ∼ *fa*', still ''*a*' is meaningful' can, and doesn't this revive the original problem in another form?[1] One possible rejoinder is that ''*a*' is meaningful', if true, is analytic, so that '*fa*' and ' ∼ *fa*' can still be contradictories; but before resting content with this rejoinder I should like to see a satisfactory analysis of meaningfulness. Another possible rejoinder is that ''*a*' is meaningful' cannot be inferred from '*fa*', but only from ''*fa*' is meaningful.' But then there is the counter-rejoinder that ''*fa*' is meaningful' follows from ''*fa*' is true,' and ''*fa*' is true' follows from '*fa*'. Paradoxes involving the word 'true,' however, are no novelty.

To make matters clearer, let us take a particular example. Consider:

   (1)   The moon is round;
   (2)   The word "round" is meaningful;
   (3)   The sentence "The moon is round" is meaningful;
   (4)   "The moon is round" is true.

Quine's paradox is then this:

   (A)   (1) ⊰ (4);
   (B)   (4) ⊰ (3);
   (C)   (3) ⊰ (2).

Hence, by the transitivity of ⊰,

   (D)   (1) ⊰ (2).

But (D) is paradoxical. Quine of course uses "paradoxical" here, as I often do myself, to mean "counter-intuitive". (This is a common, legitimate and indeed important, use of the word. Of course, those who have no philosophical intuitions do not like using the word in this sense.)

In a paper published in *Analysis*[2] I argued that there are two interpretations (or senses) of sentence (4). Namely, a sense in which

---

[1] The "original problem", which I will not discuss, was whether "*fa*" and " ∼ *fa*" are contradictories. Langford has argued that they are not on the ground that each of them entails "(∃*x*) . *fx* ∨ ∼ *fx*" and "*a* exists", which are not logically necessary.

[2] C. Lewy, "Truth and Significance", *Analysis*, vol. 8 (1947). Actually, my example there is different, but this does not affect the main point.

(A) is true but (B) is false, and a sense in which (B) is true but (A) is false. But, I argued, there is no sense of (4) in which (A) and (B) are *both* true. Hence, I concluded, Quine's paradox is solved.

To put it more fully:

	Sense 1		Sense 2
(A)	$(1) \dashv\mkern-6mu 3\ (4)$	(A)	$(1) \nvdash\mkern-9mu 3\ (4)$
(B)	$(4) \nvdash\mkern-9mu 3\ (3)^1$	(B)	$(4) \dashv\mkern-6mu 3\ (3)$
(C)	$(3) \dashv\mkern-6mu 3\ (2)$	(C)	$(3) \dashv\mkern-6mu 3\ (2)$

(I will assume that (C) is true.)

Now in his collection of essays entitled *From a Logical Point of View*,[2] Quine refers to my paper and in effect grants me that there is no paradox here and that he has made a mistake (pp. 137n, 164). He is not very explicit about the whole matter, and I shall put his views in my own words. But if I understand him correctly, he now withdraws (A) and adopts what I have just labelled the *second* interpretation (or sense) of (4). That is, he gives up the step that $(1) \dashv\mkern-6mu 3\ (4)$, but retains the step that $(4) \dashv\mkern-6mu 3\ (3)$.

In other words, he admits that the "if and only if" of Tarski's adequacy condition must *not* be interpreted as he and Carnap have interpreted it. Actually, he says, "there is no need to claim" that statements of the form:

"—" is true-in-L if and only if—,

where any one statement is written in the two blanks, are analytic (p. 137n). But he doesn't say that he himself has once done so![3]

However, Quine still seems unwilling to accept my *first* interpretation of (4). And he thus seems to imply that in asserting (A) he was simply guilty of a blunder. I think that in this he is less than fair to himself, and perhaps also less than fair to my *Analysis* paper.

To see this, let us ask: How *is* the "if and only if" of Tarski's adequacy condition to be interpreted? Tarski,[4] and now also Quine,

---

1 "$\nvdash\mkern-9mu 3$" means "does not strictly imply".

2 W. V. O. Quine, *From a Logical Point of View* (Cambridge, Mass., 1953; 2nd edn (revised), New York and Evanston, 1961).

3 Like many others, Quine uses "analytic" here (and in his original review) to mean "logically necessary". We shall discuss the relationship between the two notions later.

4 Cf. A. Tarski, "The Semantic Conception of Truth", *Philosophy and Phenomenological Research*, vol. 4 (1944). Tarski's definition of truth for formalised languages is given in A. Tarski, *Pojęcie Prawdy w Językach Nauk Dedukcyjnych* (Warsaw, 1933). German trans. (with a new *Nachwort*) in *Studia Philosophica*, vol. 1 (1936). English trans. (based on the German) in A. Tarski, *Logic, Semantics, Meta-*

interpret it to mean material equivalence (i.e. truth-functional bi-conditional). Let us discuss this.

Consider the following proposition:

(α)   The proposition expressed by the English sentence "Snow is white" is true $\equiv$ snow is white.[1]

I have formulated (α) by using the phrase "the proposition expressed by the English sentence "...""" rather than the phrase "the English sentence "...""". I have done so partly because I think this is the more correct formulation, and partly because I wish to *avoid* the objection – which is irrelevant to this discussion – that it is improper to peak of *sentences* as being true or false. Those, on the other hand, who prefer to speak of sentences as being true or false can reformulate (α) accordingly.

I think it is clear that (α) is true; but what is its truth based on? Or, to put the matter more generally, *why* is Tarski's condition (when the "if and only if" in it is interpreted to mean $\equiv$) a standard for the aedquacy of any definition of truth? Surely, the condition is not supposed to be arbitrary!

To discuss this let us consider the following propositions:

(1)   The proposition expressed by the English sentence "Snow is white" is the proposition that snow is white;

(2)   The proposition that snow is white is true;

(3)   The proposition expressed by the English sentence "Snow is white" is true;

(4)   Snow is white.[2]

Now

(A) $[(1) \,\&\, (2)] \rightarrow (3)$;

(B) $[(1) \,\&\, (3)] \rightarrow (2)$;

(C)   If (A) then $(1) \rightarrow [(2) \supset (3)]$;

(D)   If (B) then $(1) \rightarrow [(3) \supset (2)]$.[3]

---

mathematics (Oxford, 1956). Nothing that I say in this Chapter is meant to belittle the importance of Tarski's monograph as a contribution to pure logic. I think it is right to state this expressly.

[1] I use "$\equiv$" for material equivalence, "$\supset$" for material implication, "&" for conjunction and "$\vee$" for disjunction.

[2] Those who prefer to do so may reformulate (1)–(3) as follows:

      (1′) The English sentence "Snow is white" means that snow is white (and nothing else);

      (2′) That snow is white is true;

      (3′) The English sentence "Snow is white" is true.

[3] (C) and (D) are based of course on the modal principle that if $(P \,\&\, Q) \rightarrow R$, then $P \rightarrow (Q \supset R)$.

From (A), (B), (C) and (D) we get:

(E)   (1) $\dashv$ [(2) $\equiv$ (3)].

But (1) is true; and from (1) and (E) we get:

(F)   (2) $\equiv$ (3).

(F) is of course equivalent to:

(3) $\equiv$ (2),

which I will label, for a reason which will be clear shortly, (γ).

If I may digress for a moment, notice that the fact that it is *not* true that (3) $\equiv$ (2) shows conclusively that (1) is not logically necessary. For if (1) *were* logically necessary, it *would be* true that (3) $\equiv$ (2). For clearly

$$\{[(P \,\&\, Q) \dashv R] \,\&\, \sim \Diamond \sim P\} \supset (Q \dashv R).$$

And this is peculiarly obvious if we put it in the equivalent form

$$\{[P \dashv (Q \supset R)] \,\&\, \sim \Diamond \sim P\} \supset (Q \dashv R).$$

For it is obvious that anything which is entailed by a necessary proposition is itself necessary. So the absurd view of A. R. White, B. H. Medlin and J. J. C. Smart that propositions such as (1) are logically necessary can be finally dismissed.

But to return to the argument.

Notice that (γ) is still *not* what (α) – which is a particular instance of Tarski's adequacy condition – asserts. What (α) asserts is that (3) $\equiv$ (4). How do we get from (γ) to (α)? Obviously, we have to add:

(β)   (2) $\equiv$ (4).

In other words:

(γ)   (3) $\equiv$ (2);

(β)   (2) $\equiv$ (4);

therefore,

(α)   (3) $\equiv$ (4).

That is,

[(γ) $\&$ (β)] $\dashv$ (α);

hence

(β) $\dashv$ [(γ) $\supset$ (α)].

Now if (β) were *not* logically necessary it would merely be true that

(γ) $\supset$ (α);

but clearly it is also true that

(γ) $\dashv$ (α).

Hence (β) *is* logically necessary.

In other words, the following is also true:

(β')   (2) $\equiv$ (4).

And this of course is what Quine had half-seen when he said that ""*fa*" is true" follows from "*fa*"; i.e. when he asserted what in my example is premiss (A) of the alleged paradox. Only he won't accept this, and consequently won't accept my *first* interpretation of the sentence ""The moon is round" is true", since to do so would make it necessary for him to distinguish between the meaning of the phrase "the proposition that. . ." and the meaning of the phrase "the proposition expressed by the sentence". . .".

What are the consequences of all this? I think the main consequences are as follows.

1. The "semantic" conception of truth presupposes a "non-semantic" conception of truth – i.e. a conception of truth in which "true" is applied directly to propositions, and *not* to sentences. In other words, we must recognize the distinction between "the proposition that. . .is true" and "the proposition expressed by the sentence ". . ." is true".

2. Hence, we must recongize the distinction between the meaning of the phrase:

The proposition that. . .

and the meaning of the phrase:

The proposition expressed by the sentence ". . .".

3. It is clearly the *necessary* proposition (β) which gives an adequacy condition for what Tarski calls the "classical" (i.e. the correspondence) conception of truth, and *not* the contingent proposition (α).

4. Modal notions *are* involved in Quine's paradox, and they must be recognized whatever Quine may say to the contrary.

3

Reference and modality

There is something else in Quine's *From a Logical Point of View* which is highly relevant to our discussion in the previous Chapter, and is also very interesting in itself.

Quine says that the paper on "Reference and Modality" (i.e. Essay VIII in his book) has grown out of a fusion, with "sundry omissions, revisions and insertions", of "Notes on Existence and Necessity"[1] with "The Problem of Interpreting Modal Logic".[2] Now if we compare "Reference and Modality" with "Notes on Existence and Necessity", we shall notice the following insertion on p. 141 of the former:

> It would not be quite accurate to conclude that an occurrence of a name within single quotes is *never* referential.[3] Consider the statements:
>
> (6) 'Giorgione played chess' is true,
> (7) 'Giorgione' named a chess player,
>
> each of which is true or false according as the quotationless statement:
>
> (8) Giorgione played chess
>
> is true or false. Our criterion of referential occurrence makes the occurrence of the name 'Giorgione' in (8) referential, and must make the occurrences of 'Giorgione' in (6) and (7) referential by the same token, despite the presence of single quotes in (6) and (7). The point about quotation is not that it must destroy referential occurrence, but that it can (and ordinarily does) destroy referential occurrence. The examples (6) and (7) are exceptional in that the special predicates 'is true' and 'named' have the effect of undoing the single quotes – as is evident on comparison of (6) and (7) with (8).

---

[1] *Journal of Philosophy*, vol. 40 (1943).
[2] *Journal of Symbolic Logic*, vol. 12 (1947).
[3] Quine uses *single* quotes for constructing quotations.

This insertion seems to me extraordinary. It is clear, I think, that Quine is still unwilling to recognize the two senses of (6) corresponding to my two senses of (4), and is therefore unwilling to say, as I should say, that in one of them the occurrence of "Giorgione" is referential (the analogue of sense (1) of (4)) and in the other it is not referential (the analogue of sense (2) of (4)). Instead, he says that "is true" and "named" have the effect of "undoing" quotation marks. But "is true" has this effect only in my *first* interpretation of (6), and *not* in my second interpretation – and the second interpretation is the only one that Quine seemed to recognize in his (implicit) treatment of his paradox in the book!

Surely there is a big muddle in Quine's position. For one thing, according to Quine's well-known theory of quoted language, there is *no* occurrence of "Giorgione" in (7) at all. What does occur in (7) is the expression ""Giorgione"" (as opposed to "Giorgione"). Also, on Quine's theory, there is no occurrence of the name "Giorgione" in (6): in (6) the *letters* "G", "i", "o", "r", "g", "i", "o", "n" and "e" occur, in this order, within the expression ""Giorgione played chess"", i.e. within a *name* of a sentence.

Hence, the passage I have quoted from the paper on "Reference and Modality" is completely inconsistent with Quine's theory of quoted language which he first stated in *Mathematical Logic*,[1] has repeated in various other writings, and has never, so far as I know, abandoned (except implicitly in the paper which I am now discussing).

Let us, however, discuss Quine's *new* theory. In the passage which I have quoted Quine refers to "our criterion of referential occurrence". But what *is* that criterion? As a matter of fact Quine does not use this expression earlier in his article (pp. 139–40); but it seems clear that he is referring to the statement which he makes on the previous page (p. 140), namely the statement "Failure of substitutivity reveals merely that the occurrence to be supplanted is not *purely referential*...". Hence, "our criterion of referential occurrence" would seem to amount to being subject to the principle of substitutivity. But what is *that* principle? Quine states it at the very beginning of his paper when he says (p. 139):

One of the fundamental principles governing identity is that of *substitutivity* – or, as it might well be called, that of *indiscernibility*

[1] W. V. O. Quine, *Mathematical Logic* (New York, 1940; revised edn, Cambridge, Mass., 1951).

of identicals. It provides that, *given a true statement of identity, one of its two terms may be substituted for the other in any true statement and the result will be true.*

But how is the italicized part of the last sentence to be understood?

Consider:

(*a*)   "Socrates" named a philosopher;

(*b*)   Socrates is identical with the teacher of Plato.

Now it is *not* the case that the conjunction of (*a*) and (*b*) strictly implies:

(*c*)   The expression "the teacher of Plato" named a philosopher.

Yet (*a*) ≡ (*c*); and similarly (*a*) ≡ (Socrates was a philosopher); and (*a*) ≡ (the teacher of Plato was a philosopher).

Consider next:

(*d*)   The expression "the capital of England" names London;

(*e*)   The capital of England is identical with the largest city in England.

Again it is *not* the case that the conjunction of (*d*) and (*e*) strictly implies:

(*f*)   The expression "the largest city in England" names London.

Yet (*d*) ≡ (*f*), and also (*d*) ≡ (the capital of England is London), and (*d*) ≡ (the largest city in England is London).

Are we then to say that the occurrence of "Socrates" in (*a*) and that of "the capital of England" in (*d*) are purely referential? (For the sake of the argument I shall talk from now on as if it were correct to speak of the occurrence of the interior of a quotation in a sentence which contains that quotation.) On Quine's view we should have to say that they *are* purely referential, because of the material equivalence of (*a*) and (*c*) and of (*d*) and (*f*). Yet to do so would be entirely incorrect. For consider the following example:

(*g*)   The word "cat" has three letters.

Assume, as is logically possible, that all words and descriptions, in all languages, which have the same reference (i.e. denotation) as "cat" have three letters. Then compare (*g*) with:

(*h*)   The word "kot" has three letters.

On our assumption, $(g) \equiv (h)$ and the same would be true if in (g) we substituted for "cat" any word having the same reference. But would this make the occurrence of "cat" in (g) referential? No, (g) still wouldn't be about cats!

Here is a different example. Assume that all words (and descriptions), in all languages, which have the same reference as "cat" have *more than two* letters. Then consider:

(g') The word "cat" has more than two letters;

(h') The word "kot" has more than two letters.

Here it is even plainer that our assumption is logically possible: for it is, I think, actually true. On Quine's criterion, then, the occurrence of "cat" in (g'), and that of "kot" in (h'), are purely referential. This is absurd. The sentences are not about cats; they are about the word "cat" and the word "kot" respectively.

Now let us suppose that the second of the above assumptions is true, but that the first is false. Then, on Quine's criterion, the occurrence of "cat" *is* referential in (g') but is *not* referential in (g)! Hence, the occurrence of "cat" in (g) and its occurrence in (g') are radically different. This is a *reductio ad absurdum* of Quine's interpretation of the principle of substitutivity.

Notice also that Quine himself gives the example:

(A)   Giorgione was called "Giorgione" because of his size,

and says that substitution on the basis of:

(B)   Giorgione = Barbarelli

converts (A) into an equally true statement:

(C)   Barbarelli was called "Giorgione" because of his size;

and he says that in (C) "the second occurrence of the personal name is no more referential than any other occurrence within a context of quotes" (p. 140).

But on Quine's theory of quoted language there is *no* "second occurrence of the personal name" in (C) – in (C) there is only an occurrence of the expression ""Giorgione"" which is not a personal name: it is a name of the *word* "Giorgione", and a word is not a person. So that Quine not only tells us, as we have seen, that the personal name "Giorgione" occurs in (7); he also tells us that it occurs in (C) – and thus again contradicts his theory of quoted language.

Moreover, if the personal name "Giorgione" occurs in (C), then by parity of reasoning it occurs also in:

(D)   The name "Giorgione" has nine letters.

Lastly, it is clear that (C) can be reformulated as:

(C′)   "Giorgione" was used as a name for Barbarelli because of his size.

Hence Quine would have to say that whilst the "special predicate" (as he calls it) "named" has "the effect of undoing quotes", "was used as a name for" has not this effect. But then (7) can in turn be reformulated as:

(7′)   "Giorgione" was used as a name for a chess player;

and in (7′), Quine would have to say, "was used as a name for" does "undo" the quotes!

It is therefore clear that even if Quine were right in saying that in (7) there is a referential occurrence of "Giorgione", he would still not be right in implying, as he obviously does, that this is due to the fact that the special predicate "named" *always* has the effect of undoing quotes. And it is only if it *always* had this effect that Quine would have provided an explanation of the alleged referential occurrence of "Giorgione" in (7), despite the presence of quotes in it.

Let us return to (g′). Why is the occurrence of "cat" in (g′) not referential? For the following reason: given our assumption, (g′) is materially equivalent to *any* statement (Δ) which results from (g′) by the substitution for "cat" of a word having the same reference; but there is no true identity-proposition which in conjunction with (g′) *strictly implies* (Δ). And the same holds, *mutatis mutandis*, of Quine's example.

Consider:

(7)   "Giorgione" named a chess player;

(7′)   Giorgione = Barbarelli;

(7″)   "Barbarelli" named a chess player.

Quine holds that in (7) the occurrence of "Giorgione" is referential; but this is false since the conjunction of (7) and (7′) does *not* strictly imply (7″).

What, then, is the source of Quine's error in thinking that in (7) the occurrence of "Giorgione" is purely referential? I believe it is as follows. He thinks that for the occurrence of "a" in "ϕa" to be purely referential it is sufficient, and of course necessary, that the substitution for "a" of any term having the same reference (i.e. extension, denotation) as "a" be truth-preserving – be such that it *does not* lead from truth to falsehood. But I think I have shown that this is not enough: it is also necessary (and sufficient) that such substitution be *necessarily* truth-preserving – that it be *logically impossible* for it to lead from truth to falsehood.

It follows immediately that, *pace* Quine, the very criterion of referential occurrence (that is, of referential transparency) involves a modal notion.

From now on I shall say that an expression E in a sentence S is referentially transparent (or, for short, transparent) if and only if the substitution for E of any expression E' which has the same reference as E is *necessarily* truth-preserving; and I shall say that a sentence is transparent if and only if all the expressions in it are transparent. I shall say that an expression E in a sentence S is referentially opaque (or, for short, opaque) if and only if it is not transparent; and that a sentence is opaque if and only if it is not transparent.

2

I shall now discuss some of the other things which Quine says in his paper on "Reference and Modality".

Consider the following statements which he discusses:

(15)   9 is necessarily greater than 7;
(18)   The number of planets is necessarily greater than 7;
(30)   ($\exists x$) (x is necessarily greater than 7).[1]

Quine holds that according to the "strict sense" of "necessarily" (15) would be regarded as true, but (18) would be regarded as false (p. 143).

He then goes on to say (pp. 147–8) that the apparent consequence (30) of (15) raises the question: What is this number which according to (30) is necessarily greater than 7? And he continues:

According to (15), from which (30) was inferred, it was 9, that is, the number of planets; but to suppose this would conflict with the fact that (18) is false. In a word, to be necessarily greater than 7 is not a trait of a number, but depends on the manner of referring to the number.

Quine claims that we can't quantify across modal operators, i.e. that formulae such as (30) are incoherent; and although he says

---

[1] Pp. 143ff. I reproduce Quine's numbering.

I use "($\exists x$)" for the existential quantifier and "(x)" for the universal quantifier. "($\exists x$)" means "At least one object x is such that"; "(x)" means "Each object x is such that". I sometimes put the sign for the universal quantifier, without brackets and in smaller type, at the right-hand side of the sign for material equivalence.

that (15) "would be regarded as true" and that (18) "would be regarded as false", his real claim is that (15) and (18) are, like (30), incoherent too: it is only those who employ modal notions that would "regard", Quine thinks, (15) and (18) as true and false respectively.

I will now quote two other passages from "Reference and Modality". I will then also quote a passage from a later paper.

On p. 149 Quine says:

Whatever is greater than 7 is a number, and any given number x greater than 7 can be uniquely determined by any of various conditions, some of which have '$x > 7$' as a *necessary* consequence and some of which do not. One and the same number x is uniquely determined by the condition:

$$(32) \quad x = \sqrt{x} + \sqrt{x} + \sqrt{x} \neq \sqrt{x}$$

and by the condition:

$$(33) \quad \text{There are exactly } x \text{ planets,}$$

but (32) has '$x > 7$' as a necessary consequence while (33) does not. *Necessary* greaterness than 7 makes no sense as applied to a *number* x; necessity attaches only to the connection between '$x > 7$' and the particular method (32), as opposed to (33), of specifying x.

This, Quine claims,[1] is a *new* argument which avoids reference to singular terms, such as "9" and "the number of planets", and yet supports the desired conclusion – that (30) is incoherent. (He actually claims here that (30) is "meaningless".)

Later Quine says (pp. 154–5):

[The only hope of sustaining quantified modal logic] must consist in arguing or deciding that quantification into modal contexts makes sense even though any value of the variable of such a quantification be determinable by conditions that are not analytically equivalent to each other. The only hope lies in accepting the situation illustrated by (32) and (33) and insisting, despite it, that the object x in question is necessarily greater than 7. This means adopting an invidious attitude toward certain ways of uniquely specifying x, for example (33), and favoring other ways, for example (32), as somehow better revealing the "essence" of

---

[1] *Ibid.*

the object. Consequences of (32) can, from such a point of view, be looked upon as necessarily true of the object which is 9 (and is the number of the planets), while some consequences of (33) are rated still as only contingently true of that object.

Finally, I will quote a passage from a paper of Quine's entitled "Reply to Professor Marcus":

> The only course open to the champion of quantified modal logic is to meet my strictures head on: to argue in the case of 9 and the number of the planets that this number is, of itself and in-dependently of mode of specification, something that necessarily, not contingently, exceeds 7. This means adopting a frankly in-equalitarian attitude toward the various ways of specifying the number. One of the determining traits, the succeeding of 8, is counted as a necessary trait of the number. So are any traits that follow from that one, notably the exceeding of 7. Other uniquely determining traits of the number, notably its numbering the planets, are discounted as contingent traits of the number and held not to belie the fact that the number does still necessarily exceed 7.[1]

These, then, are Quine's arguments. Let us discuss them. Consider:

   (1) x = the number which succeeds 8.

(This is what Quine substitutes in the last passage which I have quoted for (32) in "Reference and Modality".)

Now (1) uniquely determines a number. By saying, rightly, that (1) has as a *necessary* consequence:

   (3) $x > 7$,

Quine has *committed* himself to acknowledging that:

   (2)   The number which succeeds 8 > 7

is a *logically necessary* proposition.

Why? Because (1) can be said to entail (3) only if the conjunction of (1) and (2) entails (3), and (2) is itself logically necessary. (By "entails" here I mean "strictly implies".)[2] For in this case (2) can be suppressed.

---

[1] *Synthèse*, vol. 13 (1961). Reprinted in W. V. O. Quine, *The Ways of Paradox and Other Essays* (New York, 1966), p. 182.

[2] As I mentioned before, until I come to discuss the relation between entailment and strict implication I shall always use "entails" to mean "strictly implies".

Now consider:

(1′) x = the number of planets.

By saying, rightly, that (1′) does *not* have (3) as a necessary consequence, Quine has *committed* himself to acknowledging that:

(2′)   The number of planets > 7

is a *contingent* proposition. For the conjunction of (1′) and (2′) entails (3) just as much as does the conjunction of (1) and (2); only here (2′), being contingent, *cannot* be suppressed.[1]

So Quine is clearly committed to recognizing the distinction between necessary propositions and contingent propositions, although in some of his writings (e.g. in "Two Dogmas of Empiricism")[2] he seems to hold that the distinction is essentially unclear, and, unless I have misunderstood him, talks as if one could do without it. Indeed, Quine is committed to recognizing the distinction as soon as he admits, as he repeatedly does, that conditions (1) and (1′) are not *analytically* equivalent. For by "not analytically equivalent" he means of course "not necessarily equivalent" – he is not trying to distinguish between "analytically equivalent" and "necessarily equivalent". And we must also notice that (2) is *not* a "logical truth" in Quine's sense: it is not "a statement which is true and remains true under all reinterpretations of its components other than the logical particles".[3] It follows immediately that Quine is committed not merely to recognizing the distinction between "logical truths" (in his sense) and truths which are not "logical": he is also committed to recognizing the distinction between necessary truths and truths that are not necessary, where "necessary" does *not* mean "*logically* true".

I may add parenthetically that Quine seems to think that the distinction between "logical particles" and particles which are not logical – on which the distinction between logical and non-logical truths (in his sense) is based – is itself arbitrary.[4] As if one could

---

[1] That Quine is *himself* saying that (1) has (3) as a necessary consequence but (1′) does not, and that he is not merely arguing that this is the position which would have to be adopted by the supporter of quantified modal logic – all this seems to me entirely obvious. To suppose otherwise would imply that, contrary to what Quine himself expressly claims, the passage which I have quoted from p. 149 of "Reference and Modality" contains *no* new argument in favour of the view that (30) is incoherent.

[2] *The Philosophical Review*, vol. 60 (1951). Reprinted in *From a Logical Point o View*.   [3] *Ibid.* pp. 22–3.

[4] E.g. in *Mathematical Logic* he talks of a "superficial" distinction between logical truths and truths of other kinds (pp. 1ff.).

take "red" or "blue" to be logical particles, and "not" and "and" to be descriptive particles! (Why hasn't anybody tried to do this?)

As a matter of fact, the idea that the distinction between logical and non-logical particles *may be arbitrary to some extent*, was stated explicitly by Tarski in his paper "On the Concept of Logical Consequence".[1] But Tarski himself admits that the distinction is certainly not *entirely* arbitrary, and points out that if, e.g., we were not to include among logical particles the implication sign or the quantifiers, then his definition of logical consequence would lead to results which obviously contradict ordinary intuitions.[2]

But to return to Quine. He would presumably have to claim that although we should all, including himself, *unhesitatingly* say that (2) is necessary (where "necessary" does not mean "*logically* true"), and *unhesitatingly* say that (2') is *not* necessary, this is still due to our acceptance of some arbitrary distinction. But I have no idea *what* distinction this is supposed to be, and I have therefore no idea how he would support such a claim.

Let us return to (1), (2) and (3), and let us add:

    (4)   (2) is necessary.

Now so far as I can see, (4) entails:

    (5)   The number which succeeds 8 is necessarily greater than 7.

But (5) entails:

    (6) $(\exists x)$ (x is necessarily greater than 7).

(Quine accepts the Russellian analysis of "the".)

But if so, then, since (4) is true, (6) is also true. And (6) is of course identical with Quine's (30) which he claims to be incoherent (or "meaningless").

Now let us return to:

    (2')   The number of planets > 7,

and let us add:

    (7)   (2') is not necessary.

If (6) and (7) are both true, as they are, they cannot conflict. Moreover, if we ask, with Quine, "What is this number which,

---

[1] English trans. by J. H. Woodger in A. Tarski, *Logic, Semantics, Metamathematics.* See esp. pp. 418–19.

[2] I am translating from the Polish version, "O Pojęciu Wynikania Logicznego", *Przegląd Filozoficzny*, vol. 39 (1936). Woodger's translation has "ordinary usage" instead of "ordinary intuitions". This positivist metamorphosis occurs also in the German version of the paper (which Woodger used for his translation) published in *Actualités Scientifiques et Industrielles*, vol. 394 (Paris, 1936).

according to (6), is necessarily greater than 7?", and answer "It is the number 9, that is, the number of planets", this will not conflict with the fact that (2′) is not necessary. But Quine thinks that it *will* conflict with the fact that his (18) is false. He has, however, given no reason for supposing that (18) is false. I suggest that he thinks (18) false because he confuses:

    (α)   The proposition that the number of planets is greater than 7 is necessary

with

    (β)   The number of planets is necessarily greater than 7.
But (α) and (β) are different: (α) is false, but (β) is true.

    I shall call propositions such as (α) *de dicto* modal propositions, and propositions such as (β) *de re* modal propositions. It follows immediately that a *de re* modal proposition does not always entail the corresponding *de dicto* modal proposition.

    (Actually, to say that Quine confuses (β) with (α) is in a way too fair to him. He confuses (β) not with (α), but with (γ) "The proposition expressed by the sentence "the number of planets is greater than 7" is necessary". But I have already gone into this in another connexion.)

    If all this is right, then "being necessarily greater than 7" *is* a property of the number 9: necessity does *not*, as Quine claims, attach only to the connexion between "$x > 7$" and the particular methods, e.g. (32) and (1), of specifying the number.

    Hence, what Quine says about the occurrence of "9" in (15) is wrong. Consider again:

    (15)   9 is necessarily greater than 7
and add:

    (24)   The number of planets = 9.[1]
The substitution in (15) of "the number of planets" for "9" does *not* lead from truth to falsehood:

    (18)   The number of planets is necessarily greater than 7
is *not* false. Quine's difficulty was that (15) would be "regarded" as true but (18) would be "regarded" as false. But (18) is *not* false, and this is the solution of Quine's problem.

    Hence there is also no reason to think that (30) is incoherent – we have in fact seen that (30) is true.

    Now Quine was aware when he wrote "Reference and Modality" that his position can be challenged by saying that he confuses (α)

---

[1] Quine's numbering.

with (β). For essentially the same point was made, although in a somewhat different way, by A. F. Smullyan in his paper on "Modality and Description",[1] to which Quine refers.

Quine thought, however, that he could re-argue for the meaninglessness of (30) in a way which avoids reference to singular terms. But the new argument does not succeed: for it consists in no more than claiming that we are being inequalitarian in considering that (1) reveals better the "essence" of the number 9 than does $(1')$.

But *is* this attitude inequalitarian? Clearly not. For a specification which *entails* with respect to a property which necessarily belongs to a number that it does belong to it, is clearly more fundamental than a specification which does not entail this.

Moreover, the conjunction of (1) and (5) entails:

$(3')$ x is necessarily greater than 7.

Assuming that (5) is itself necessary, we can say that (1) entails $(3')$. And that (5) *is* necessary follows from the conjunction of:

(i) (4) entails (5)

and

(ii) (4) is necessary.

(I shall argue in favour of (ii) later when I come to discuss Lewis's system S4.)

If all this is correct, i.e. if (1) entails $(3')$, then specification (1) entails not only with respect to a property which necessarily belongs to 9 that it does belong to it: it entails also that that property *necessarily* belongs to 9. And surely a specification which entails with respect to a property which necessarily belongs to a number that it does necessarily belong to it, is more fundamental than a specification which does not entail this.

Hence, to favour (1) against $(1')$ is not to adopt an inequalitarian attitude.

And, finally, Quine himself adopts it, and he is therefore himself an "essentialist": for by claiming, rightly, that (1) entails (3) whilst $(1')$ does not entail (3), he is committed, as I have already pointed out, to maintaining that (2) is necessary and that $(2')$ is contingent. So he himself "counts" the trait of succeeding 8 as a necessary trait of 9 and that of its numbering the planets as a contingent trait! Moreover, he explicitly admits that specifications (32) and (33) are not analytically equivalent, and would of course have to admit that specifications (1) and $(1')$ are also not analytically equivalent. But

---

[1] *Journal of Symbolic Logic*, vol. 13 (1948).

there can be no doubt that he would agree that specifications (1) and (32) *are* analytically equivalent. So Quine is quite able to distinguish between those traits of the number 9 which are necessary traits of it and those of its traits which are only contingent: the necessary (i.e. essential) traits of 9 are those and only those which are given by specifications analytically equivalent to (32). All the other traits of 9 are contingent (i.e. accidental).

It seems to me that this constitutes a conclusive refutation of Quine's view that "essentialism" is an invidious, inequalitarian, arbitrary attitude. He *says* that he finds this attitude "uncongenial",[1] but in fact he holds it himself! And it should now be recalled that he admits, both in the second passage which I have quoted from "Reference and Modality" and in the passage which I have quoted from "Reply to Professor Marcus", that the only hope of sustaining quantified modal logic lies in "arguing or deciding" that quantification into modal contexts makes sense even though any value of the variable of such a quantification be determinable by conditions that are not analytically equivalent to each other. This means of course that the only hope of sustaining quantified modal logic lies in *rejecting* Quine's theory that necessity depends on the manner of referring to an object, and *accepting* the "essentialist" theory that some properties of an object are essential to it and others only accidental. And this, as I think I have shown, is the theory Quine is himself committed to, though he doesn't realize it.

3

Let us recall that Quine agrees that (1) entails (3), and that this, as I have shown, presupposes that (2) is necessary. Now Quine might argue that the necessity of (2) is *based* on the fact that (3) is a necessary consequence of (1). But to argue thus would be to put the cart before the horse. For, as I have already pointed out, what justifies us in saying that (1) entails (3) is that the *conjunction* of (1) and (2) entails (3); hence (2) entails that (1) materially implies (3); but since (2) is necessary, and what is entailed by a necessary proposition is itself necessary, we can conclude that (1) entails (3).

In other words, it is the *truth* of (2) that justifies us in asserting that (1) *materially implies* (3), and it is the *necessity* of (2) that justifies us in asserting that it is *necessarily true* that (1) materially implies

---

[1] *The Ways of Paradox and Other Essays*, p. 182.

(3), i.e. in asserting that (1) strictly implies (3).[1] To suppose that it is the last which justifies us in asserting that (2) is necessary would be as absurd as to suppose that it is the fact that (1) materially implies (3) which justifies us in asserting that (2) is true! Hence, it is the necessity of (2) which is here the basic matter. In other words, the existence of a necessary connexion between (1) and (3), i.e. the fact that (1) entails (3), is derived from the necessity of (2) and not vice versa. Thus necessity attaches primarily to the *proposition* (2), and only derivatively to the connexion between "$x > 7$" and the particular method, viz. method (1), of specifying x.

There remains the following point. I have said that Quine confuses:

(α)   The proposition that the number of planets is greater than 7 is necessary

with:

(β)   The number of planets is necessarily greater than 7.

Now as Smullyan has pointed out,[2] (α) can be expressed as:

$$\sim \Diamond \sim [(\exists x) (\phi_\zeta \equiv_z \zeta = x \ \& \ Fx)]$$

whilst (β) can be expressed as:

$$(\exists x) [\phi_\zeta \equiv_z \zeta = x \ \& \sim \Diamond \sim (Fx)],$$

where ϕ stands for "numbers the planets", and F for "is greater than 7".

Smullyan has also pointed out, and this is very important, that whilst (α) is logically impossible, (β) is true *but contingent*.

But now consider:

(β')   The number which succeeds 8 is necessarily greater than 7.

(β') is necessary. Hence, the substitution of "identicals" may change the modality (i.e. the modal value) of (β'), but *not* its truth-value.

In other words, the conjunction of:

(β')   The number which succeeds 8 is necessarily greater than 7

and

(γ)   The number which succeeds 8 = the number of planets

entails:

(β)   The number of planets is necessarily greater than 7;

---

[1] I repeat that I am using "entails" to mean "strictly implies".

[2] Smullyan's examples are in fact slightly different, but this does not affect the essential point.

but the conjunction of (β') and (γ) does *not* entail that (β) is itself a necessary proposition (which it isn't): for the identity-proposition (γ) is itself a contingent proposition.

To conclude. Propositions of the form (α) are, if true, necessary; propositions of the form (β) are sometimes necessary, sometimes contingent. A proposition of the form (β) – let us call it a (β)-proposition – is necessary if the corresponding proposition of the form (α) is true; otherwise it is contingent. A substitution based on a *contingent* identity-proposition may well alter the modality of a (β)-proposition; a substitution based on a *necessary* identity-proposition will *not* do so; and never, of course, will a substitution based on a (true) identity-proposition, be it a necessary or a contingent one, alter the *truth-value* of a (β)-proposition.

Thus there *is* something which is necessarily greater than 7 – the number 9, that is, the number of planets.

It follows that we can coherently quantify into modal contexts. It also follows that whilst *de dicto* modal statements are referentially opaque, *de re* modal statements are referentially transparent: this latter point Quine fails to see owing to his confusion of *de re* statements with *de dicto* statements.

4

External and internal relations

I shall now try to show that G. E. Moore, although he did believe that objects possessed some properties essentially and others only accidentally, also in effect confused *de re* statements with *de dicto* statements. I shall try to show that in his important and influential paper on "External and Internal Relations" he confuses two quite different accounts of the notion of an internal property (or relation), and that this confusion is based on a failure to distinguish between "Necessarily *Fa*" and "*a* is necessarily *F*", that is, between *de dicto* and *de re* statements.

Moore's paper was originally published in the *Proceedings of the Aristotelian Society* for 1919–20.[1] In 1922 it was reprinted with various changes in his *Philosophical Studies*,[2] and it is in the latter form that the paper is best known. In the Preface to the book Moore says that the changes made in this paper are not due to any change in his views, but to the fact that in the original version he used symbols taken from *Principia Mathematica*, and used them without fully explaining their meaning; that those symbols are difficult for printers to reproduce; and that he therefore thought it better, on this occasion, to use another set of symbols and to explain them more fully. He also adds that he has taken the opportunity of rewriting some parts in which the symbols in question occur in order to make some points clearer than they originally were.

In fact however, as we shall see, the changes are more substantial than Moore seems to have realized. I shall therefore have to refer to both versions of the paper.

I shall begin with two quotations. The first is as follows:

Let us take as an example the relational property which we assert to belong to a visual sense-datum when we say of it that it has

---

[1] Vol. 20 (1919–20). Hereafter abbreviated *PAS*.
[2] G. E. Moore, *Philosophical Studies* (London, 1922).

another visual sense-datum as a spatial part: the assertion, for instance, with regard to a coloured patch half of which is red and half yellow: "This whole patch contains this patch" (where "this patch" is a proper name for the red half). It is here, I think, quite plain that, in a perfectly clear and intelligible sense, we can say that any whole, which had not contained that red patch, could not have been identical with the whole in question: that from the proposition with regard to any term[1] whatever that it does not contain *that* particular patch it *follows* that that term is *other* than the whole in question – though *not* necessarily that it is qualitatively different from it. *That* particular whole could not have existed without having that particular patch for a part.[2]

The second quotation is this:

[The dogma of internal relations] implies, in fact, quite generally, that any term[3] which does in fact have a particular relational property could not have existed without having that property. And in saying this it obviously flies in the face of common sense. It seems quite obvious that in the case of many relational properties which things have, the fact that they have them is *a mere matter of fact*: that the things in question *might* have existed without having them.[4]

It seems to me clear from these passages that *one* account suggested by Moore is that a property is an internal, that is, an essential,[5] property of an object if and only if the object could not have existed without having that property. That is, that from the object's existence its possession of the property logically follows.[6]

So let us say provisionally:

(α') Assuming that ϕ is a first-order property and that existence is *not* a first-order property,[7]

ϕ is an internal property of A if and only if

A exists $\dashv$ ϕA.

It is clear, however, that (α') will do only if "A" is a proper name. Why? Because, as we have seen in the last Chapter, "being greater

---

[1] He means *object*, not *term*.   [2] *PAS*, p. 50; *Philosophical Studies*, pp. 287–8.

[3] He means *object*, not *term*.   [4] *PAS*, p. 51; *Philosophical Studies*, pp. 288–9.

[5] It is obvious that "internal" and "external", as Moore uses them, are synonymous with "essential" and "accidental" respectively.

[6] If I understand him rightly, this is the account attributed to Moore by A. Plantinga in his able paper "De Re et De Dicto", *Noûs*, vol. 3, 1969.

[7] Otherwise existence would always be an internal property.

than 7" *is* an essential (i.e., in Moore's terminology, "internal")
property of the number of planets; yet "The number of planets
exists" does *not* entail[1] "The number of planets is greater than 7".

Let us therefore revise (α') to read:

(α)   Assuming that ϕ is a first-order property, that existence
is *not* a first-order property, *and that "A" is a proper name*,
ϕ is an internal property of A if and only if
A exists $\dashv3\ \phi A$;

and when "A" is a definite description, ϕ is an internal property of
A if and only if the following condition is satisfied:

If the object uniquely described by "A" *were* given a proper
name, "A'", then it *would be* true that ϕ is an internal property of
A' in the sense just defined; i.e. it would be true that
A' exists $\dashv3\ \phi A'$.

(I am again assuming that ϕ is a first-order property, and that
existence is not a first-order property.)

We can now proceed as follows. We can say, I think:

A is necessarily ϕ if and only if (1) ϕA *and* (2) ϕ is an internal
property of A (as "internal property" is defined by (α)).

We have thus given a truth-condition for *de re* statements. That
is, a *de re* statement is equivalent to the joint assertion that an object
has a certain property and that that property is internal to it.
Alternatively, we can say, I think:

A is necessarily ϕ if and only if (1) A exists *and* (2) ϕ is an
internal property of A.

The necessity for the conjunct "ϕA" (or "A exists") arises in the
following way. One might well wish to assert

(A)   Russell is necessarily a son of Lord and Lady Amberley.

For it is at least plausible to suppose that "being a son of Lord and
Lady Amberley" is an internal property of Russell. That is, it seems
plausible to suppose that

(B)   Russell exists $\dashv3$ Russell is a son of Lord and Lady
Amberley.

But (B) alone does not entail (A) since (B) is itself necessary whilst
(A) is contingent.

2

Unfortunately, Moore goes on to give a totally different account of
the concept of an internal property. Namely he goes on to say:

---

[1] I use "entails" in this Chapter, as before, to mean "strictly implies".

The assertion with regard to a particular term[1] A and a particular relational property ϕ, which A actually has, that ϕ is internal to A means then: $(x): \sim \phi x$. ent . $x \neq$ A.[2] And this is, of course, logically equivalent to: $(x): x =$ A . ent . ϕx; ....[3]

He also puts this (but in the *PAS* version only, p. 55) by saying that those and only those values of ϕ are internal properties for which the following proposition is true:

$(x, y) \therefore \phi x: \supset : \sim \phi y$. ent . $y \neq x$.

And on pp. 302–3 of *Philosophical Studies* he actually says (he puts it in a slightly different way in the *PAS* version, p. 57, but the substance is the same):

> We can say that ϕA is itself a necessary truth, if and only if the universal proposition "$(x =$ A$) \supset \phi x$"[4] (which, as we have seen, follows from ϕA) is a necessary truth: that is to say, if and only if $(x =$ A$)$ entails ϕx. With this definition, what the dogma of internal relations asserts is that in every case in which a given thing actually has a given relational property, the fact that it has that property is a necessary truth; whereas what I am asserting is that, if the property in question is an "internal" property, then the fact in question will be a necessary truth, whereas if the property in question is "external", then the fact in question will be a mere "matter of fact".[5]

Let me first explain this. As is well known, Moore in the paper in question makes the important point that if $(P \& Q) \dashv R$, then $P \dashv (Q \supset R)$, but that it is not *in general* true that if $(P \& Q) \dashv R$, then $P \supset (Q \dashv R)$.[6] This of course is right. But the use which he makes of it in the present account of internal properties is as follows. He takes ϕx for P, $\sim \phi y$ for Q, and $y \neq x$ for R; he

---

1 He means *object*, not *term*.
2 "ent" is an abbreviation for "entails"; "$\neq$" means "is not identical with".
3 *PAS*, p. 54. A revised version of this passage occurs in *Philosophical Studies*, p. 297. Unfortunately in the revised version of the paper Moore omits the quantifiers throughout.
4 Of course, there is *no* universal proposition here: Moore has left out the universal quantifier; but let us disregard this.
5 I have altered Moore's symbolism in this passage to conform to that used in the *PAS* version of the paper.
6 I believe that Moore was the first philosopher to make this point in modern times; in effect therefore he showed that the deduction theorem will not hold in modal logic in a way analogous to that in which it holds in truth-functional logic.

points out that it is *always* true that

    (*a*) $(\phi x \,\&\, \sim \phi y) \dashv\!\!\!\dashv\!\!\!\vdash (y \neq x)$;

but that it is not *in general* true that

    (*b*) $\phi x \supset (\sim \phi y \dashv\!\!\!\dashv\!\!\!\vdash y \neq x)$;

and he says that internal properties are those and only those properties for which (*b*) *is* true.

This is what I shall call Moore's *second* account of the concept of an internal property. And I shall try to show that this account is entirely different from his first account.

Consider:

    (A) A is necessarily ϕ;

    (B) ϕ is an internal property of A (where this is understood in the sense of definition (α));

    (C) $(x)\,[\sim \phi x \dashv\!\!\!\dashv\!\!\!\vdash (x \neq A)]$ (i.e. ϕ is an internal property of A in the sense of Moore's *second* definition).

Since (A) entails (B), we get that if (B) entailed (C), then (A) would entail (C); but (A) does not entail (C); hence (B) does not entail (C). Hence (B) and (C) are different.

To show that (A) does not *entail* (C), it is of course enough to show that (A) does not *materially imply* (C). And it does not. For:

    (1) The number of planets is necessarily greater than 7

does not materially imply

    (2) (It is not the case that the number of books on this desk is greater than 7) $\dashv\!\!\!\dashv\!\!\!\vdash$ (the number of books on this desk $\neq$ the number of planets).

Why? Because (2) is simply false, and it is false precisely because (1), although true, is contingent.

In other words, Moore's two definitions are quite different, and (C) is *not* a necessary condition for "ϕ is an internal property of A" in the sense of Moore's *first* definition. What, then, *is* (C) a necessary condition for? I think (C) is a necessary (and sufficient) condition for something quite different, namely "It is necessary that ϕA" (where "A" is a proper name or a definite description); and I think therefore that Moore confuses in his paper *de re* with *de dicto* modal statements.

Moreover, the fact that Moore confuses his two different accounts of the concept of an internal property is clear from the very first passage which I have quoted from his paper. For already in that passage he tells us two things which he does not distinguish from each other: he tells us, with respect to his coloured patch half of which is red and half yellow, (1) that that particular whole patch could not have existed without having that particular red patch for a part; and (2) that we can say ("in a perfectly clear and intelligible sense") that any whole which had not contained that red patch could not have been identical with the whole in question. And he immediately goes on to identify this latter assertion, i.e. (2), with the assertion that from the proposition with regard to any object whatever that it does not contain that particular patch it *follows* that that object is other than the whole in question. It seems clear that (1), which suggests what I have called his *first* account, is continued in the second passage that I have quoted from the paper whilst (2), which suggests what I have called his *second* account, is continued, and much more fully developed, in the other passages that I have quoted.

It is this latter, incorrect, account, which is in fact stressed in the paper.

It may be thought that although Moore's second account of the concept of an internal property is different from his first account, it is none the less quite coherent. But it is not. For consider:

(*a*) The proposition expressed by the English sentence "There is no brother who is not male" is necessary;

(*b*) The last proposition asserted by John before he left the room is not necessary;

(*c*) The last proposition asserted by John before he left the room ≠ the proposition expressed by the English sentence "There is no brother who is not male".

Clearly, the conjunction of (*a*) and (*b*) entails (*c*). But it is *false* that (*a*) $\supset$ [(*b*) $\rightarrow\!\!\!3$ (*c*)]. For (*a*), although true, is contingent; and hence (*b*) does *not* entail (*c*).

It follows that on Moore's second definition we should have to say that "being necessary" is not an internal property of the proposition expressed by the English sentence "There is no brother who is not male". But on this very definition "being necessary" *is* an internal property of the proposition that there is no brother who is not male. But these propositions are identical – so Moore is led into contradicting Leibniz's law.[1]

It may however be suggested that Moore's second definition can be saved by amending it as follows.

Assuming that "*A*" is a proper name and ϕ is a first-order

---

[1] I mean, of course, the law of the indiscernibility of identicals.

property, ϕ is an internal property of A if and only if $(x)\,[\sim \phi x \rightarrow 3$ $(x \neq A)]$; and when "A" is a definite description (and ϕ a first-order property), ϕ is an internal property of A if and only if it is the case that if the object uniquely described by "A" were given a proper name, "A'", then it *would* be true that $(x)\,[\sim \phi x \rightarrow 3$ $(x \neq A')]$.

With this amendment the above example won't go through. But the amendment still won't do for then only an object that exists *necessarily* will be capable of having internal properties. For example, "being a son of Lord and Lady Amberley" will not be an internal property of Russell. And Moore certainly wished to attribute internal properties to objects which exist contingently as well as to those which exist necessarily.

There is one final problem which I must discuss. I said in the previous Chapter that a *de re* statement does not always entail the corresponding *de dicto* statement. For example,

(β)   The number of planets is necessarily greater than 7
does not entail

(α)   Necessarily, the number of planets is greater than 7.
(On the other hand, since I am using "entails" to mean strictly implies, it follows, assuming that if a *de dicto* proposition is true, then it is itself necessary, that "9 is necessarily greater than 7" entails "Necessarily, 9 is greater than 7".)

But now does a *de dicto* statement always entail the corresponding *de re* statement? Clearly not: it has, I think, often been pointed out that, e.g.,

(A)   Necessarily, there is a number which numbers the planets
does not entail

(B)   There is a number such that it necessarily numbers the planets.
For (A) is true whilst (B) is false.

It may be thought, however, that if a *de dicto* statement is of the form "Necessarily ϕA", *where "A" is a proper name or a definite description*, then it does entail the corresponding *de re* statement. But this is not so. For consider:

(1)   It is necessary that the number which numbers men numbers rational animals,
and
(2)   The number which numbers men necessarily numbers rational animals.

(1) is true, but (2) is false. (1) is true because

    (3)   The number which numbers men numbers rational animals

is a conjunction of: at least one number numbers men, at most one number numbers men, and there is no number which numbers men and does not number rational animals; and each of these conjuncts is necessary. But clearly (2) is false since it is not true of any number whatever that *it* necessarily numbers rational animals.

It may therefore seem that one of the arguments which I used against Quine in the previous Chapter is fallacious. Namely the argument that

    (4)   It is necessary that the number which succeeds 8 is greater than 7

entails

    (5)   The number which succeeds 8 is necessarily greater than 7.

I think, however, that (4) does entail (5); and I think so for the following reason. It seems to me that a *de dicto* statement of the form "Necessarily ϕA", where "A" is a proper name or a definite description, does entail the corresponding *de re* statement ("A is necessarily ϕ"), provided that the *de dicto* statement in question satisfies also the following condition, namely that if "A" is a definite description, then *falling under it* is an internal property of the object thus described.[1]

Let me explain this more fully. Compare (1) above with (4). It is clearly *not* an internal property of whatever number numbers men (say, the number 2,000m) that it falls under the description "the number which numbers men"; but it *is* an internal property of the number 9 that it falls under the description "the number which succeeds 8". I believe that if this further condition is satisfied, then a *de dicto* statement does entail the corresponding *de re* statement.

3

Throughout this Chapter I have identified entailment with strict implication, and hence have taken Moore's "ent" to mean " $\dashv$ ". But in view of the fact that in the paper in question he does not attempt to distinguish between them,[2] this is legitimate. Moreover, it seems clear that my main criticism of Moore would not be affected by any

---

[1] I am of course using "internal property" in the sense of definition (α).
[2] See also below.

such distinction (assuming, of course, that the distinction still makes strict implication a necessary condition for entailment).

There is another matter which it may not be out of place to mention at this point. It is well known that Moore introduced the word "entails" into philosophy as a technical term in the paper which I have been discussing.

But it seems not to be well known that in the *PAS* version of the paper there occurs, on p. 58, the following passage which Moore altered for the *Philosophical Studies* version:

> It may be held [...] that though ϕA . ent . ψA does not mean simply ϕA . $\supset$. ψA, yet what it does mean is simply the conjunction "ϕA . $\supset$. ψA, *and* this proposition is an instance of a true formal implication" (the phrase "formal implication" being understood in Mr Russell's sense, in which $(x):\phi x$. $\supset$. ψx asserts a formal implication). This view as to what ϕA . ent . ψA means has, for instance, if I understand him rightly, been asserted by Mr. O. Strachey in *Mind*, N.S., 93; since he asserts that, in his opinion, this is what Professor C. I. Lewis means by "ϕA *strictly* implies ψA," and undoubtedly what Professor Lewis means by this is what I mean by ϕA . ent . ψA. And the same view has been frequently suggested (though I do not know that he has actually asserted it) by Mr Russell himself (e.g., [in] *Principia Mathematica* [vol. 1], p. 21).

Moore then says that it appears to him perfectly obvious that this view is untrue.

In the *Philosophical Studies* version (p. 304) the words from the semi-colon to the end of the sentence, that is, the fragment involving C. I. Lewis, are deleted.

This deletion may suggest that already by the beginning of 1922 Moore wished to distinguish between entailment and strict implication.[1] This of course is possible; but I have no other evidence for it, and on the whole I am inclined to think that Moore deleted this fragment of the sentence because by 1922 he had realized that Strachey did not assert that by strict implication Lewis *meant* formal implication, but rather that this is what Lewis *ought* to have meant.[2]

[1] The Preface to *Philosophical Studies* is dated January 1922.
[2] This part of Strachey's paper is thoroughly confused. See O. Strachey, "Mr Russell and Some Recent Criticisms of his Views", *Mind*, vol. 24 (1915).

In any case, from what Moore says in the deleted part of the sentence, taken together with his statement that it seems to him obvious that entailment is different

4

I have repeatedly claimed that some identity-statements are contingent and I have given examples of such statements. What, then, are we to say about the following argument discussed by Kripke:

(1) $(x,y)[(x = y) \supset (Fx \supset Fy)]$;
(2) $(x)\,\square\,(x = x)$;
(3) $(x,y)(x = y) \supset [\square\,(x = x) \supset \square\,(x = y)]$

is a substitution instance of (1); and from (2) and (3) there follows:

(4) $(x,y)[(x = y) \supset \square\,(x = y)]$?[1]

I am not sure that I understand Kripke's answer; but my own (possibly the same as his) is as follows.

I believe that (4) is all right; but it is wrong to interpret it as saying that all identity-statements are necessary. What (4) says is that for all x and y, if $x = y$, then it is necessary that $x = y$. This only means that, for all x and y, if $x = y$, then y has the property of being necessarily identical with x – which it has since x has it. In effect (4) is a different way of saying that everything is identical with itself.

We should also notice the following.

(A) $\square\,(\text{Napoleon} = \text{Napoleon})$;
(B) Napoleon = the victor of Austerlitz,

but

(C) $\sim \square\,(\text{Napoleon} = \text{the victor of Austerlitz})$.

(A), (B) and (C) are all true, but this is all right and doesn't violate Leibniz's law: for it would be nonsensical to suppose that it is a property of Napoleon that the proposition that Napoleon is identical with Napoleon is logically necessary. The necessity of that proposition is a property of *it*, and not of Napoleon. What is a property of Napoleon is that he is necessarily identical with whoever has the property that he and he alone commanded the troops that won at Austerlitz (if there is such a person – as in fact there is); and this, of course, is also a property of anything identical with Napoleon.

from formal implication, it follows immediately that Strachey could not have been right in asserting that by strict implication Lewis meant formal implication.

I think Moore must have seen this when he came to revise the paper for *Philosophical Studies*.

[1] S. Kripke, "Identity and Necessity" in M. Munitz (ed.), *Identity and Individuation* (New York, 1971), p. 136.

I use here "$\square$" to mean the same as "$\sim \lozenge \sim$", i.e. "it is logically necessary that".

That is, (C) is true and therefore its negation:

(D) $\square$ (Napoleon = the victor of Austerlitz)

is false.

What is true is:

(E)   Napoleon is necessarily identical with the victor of Austerlitz.

(E) is a *de re* statement which is *contingently* true and means:

(E′) $(\exists x)\{[z$ commanded the troops that won at Austerlitz $\equiv_z (z = x)]$ & $\square (x = $ Napoleon$)\}$.

In other words, (3) in Kripke's argument is a substitution instance of (1) only if (3) is so interpreted that "$\square (x = x)$" and "$\square (x = y)$" are *de re* statements, and not *de dicto* statements, and mean, respectively, that x is necessarily identical with x, and that x is necessarily identical with y. That is to say, (3) is a substitution instance of (1) only if (3) is so interpreted that of the following two propositions, which I will label (3′) and (3″), (3′) *is* a substitution instance of (3) but (3″) is *not*:

(3′)   (Napoleon = the victor of Austerlitz) $\supset$ [(Napoleon is necessarily identical with Napoleon) $\supset$ (Napoleon is necessarily identical with the victor of Austerlitz)];

(3″)   (Napoleon = the victor of Austerlitz) $\supset$ [(the proposition that Napoleon is identical with Napoleon is necessary) $\supset$ (the proposition that Napoleon is identical with the victor of Austerlitz is necessary)].

In brief, "Napoleon is necessarily identical with Napoleon" is a substitution instance of Fx; but "the proposition that Napoleon is identical with Napoleon is necessary" is *not*. And the same holds of "Napoleon is necessarily identical with the victor of Austerlitz", "the proposition that Napoleon is identical with the victor of Austerlitz is necessary" and Fy.

5

Necessity and convention

I

Let us now return to Wisdom's three propositions discussed in Chapter 1:

    (1)   "Vixen" means the same as "female fox";

    (2)   "Vixen" means female fox;

    (3)   A vixen may be defined as a female fox.

For reasons which will be clearer later I will express proposition (3) by the sentence:

    The concept of being a vixen is identical with the concept of being a female fox.

And from now on when I use the numeral "3" as a label for a sentence, it will be a label for this.

    Another way of expressing the proposition would be by saying:

    To be a vixen is to be a female fox.

    It doesn't matter which sentence we take, and my reformulation will not do Wisdom the slightest injustice: in fact it will make his view, if anything, a little more plausible. In any case, as I pointed out in Chapter 1, Wisdom explicitly admits that to determine which proposition is expressed by any of his three sentences one must explain the *use* of that sentence.

    How, then, are we to explain the relevant use of sentence (3)? We must do so more fully than he does himself – all that *he* says is that he is so using it that in order to understand it a man must understand both the meaning of the word "vixen" and the meaning of the expression "female fox".

    I will explain his intended use of sentence (3) as follows.

Explanation of Wisdom's use of (3)

X understands sentence (3) in the use with which Wisdom is concerned if and only if

    (A°)   *X* understands the expression "the concept of being a...";

    (A″)   *X* understands the word "vixen";

    (B″)   *X* understands the expression "female fox";

    (C″)   *X* understands the expression "is identical with";

    (D″)   *X* understands the syntax of (3).

Wisdom, as I have just pointed out, gives only conditions (A″) and (B″); but clearly the other three conditions are also necessary.

The first two questions I shall discuss are:

    Does (3) entail (1)?

    Does (3) entail (2)?

I am still identifying entailment with strict implication.

Well, does (3) entail (1)? and does (3) entail (2)? The answer is "No".

First argument. (3) is logically necessary (as Wisdom himself would admit: one of his main purposes was to explain the necessity of necessary propositions); but (1) and (2) are both contingent.

It follows immediately that (3) does not entail (1), and that (3) does not entail (2): for a necessary proposition cannot entail a contingent proposition.

This can be proved as follows:

    (*a*)   If *A* entails *B*, then ∼ *B* entails ∼ *A*.

    (*b*)   If *A* is contingent, then ∼ *A* is contingent.

    (*c*)   If *A* is necessary, then ∼ *A* is impossible.

The first premiss cannot be disputed,[1] and so far as I know the other two premisses are accepted by all modal logicians.

Now assume that a necessary proposition *P* entails a contingent proposition *Q*. Then, by (*a*) ∼ *Q* entails ∼ *P*; but by (*b*) ∼ *Q* is contingent; and by (*c*) ∼ *P* is impossible. It thus follows from our assumption that a contingent proposition, ∼ *Q*, entails an impossible proposition, ∼ *P*.

I think this would be generally accepted as a formal proof that a necessary proposition cannot entail a contingent one; for otherwise a contingent proposition would entail an impossible one. And this is absurd since if a proposition *P* entails an impossible proposition *Q*, this constitutes a proof that *P* is itself impossible.

Second argument. As I have pointed out before, both (1) and (2) entail that the word "vixen" has a meaning in English; but (3) entails nothing whatever about English. It follows immediately that (3) does not entail (1), and that (3) does not entail (2).

We can also put this argument in another way. It is obviously

---

[1] I repeat that "entails" means here "strictly implies".

logically possible that (3) be true but (1) and (2) false. Indeed, this would be the case if English did not exist.

We must now turn to the two remaining questions: Does (1) entail (3)? Does (2) entail (3)? But before doing so, I wish to point out a fact of some importance. We have just seen that a necessary proposition cannot entail a contingent proposition. There is, however, no analogous formal argument for supposing that a contingent proposition cannot entail a necessary proposition. Indeed, if there were such an argument it would follow immediately that entailment cannot be identified with strict implication![1] But there is no such formal argument. Wisdom and others use the following fallacious argument: "If a contingent proposition P entailed a necessary proposition Q, then $\sim Q$ would entail $\sim P$; but then an *a priori* proposition would entail a proposition which is not *a priori*; and this is impossible".[2] But there is nothing impossible about it. Wisdom and a number of other philosophers use "*a priori*" and "necessary" ambiguously. If "*a priori*" means "necessarily true", then an *a priori* proposition cannot entail a proposition which is not *a priori*. But if "*a priori*" means "*either* necessarily true *or* necessarily false" – as it must mean in Wisdom's argument if $\sim Q$ there is to be called "*a priori*" – then there is no reason whatever to suppose that an *a priori* proposition cannot entail a proposition which is not *a priori*. At least Wisdom has not produced any such reason. This second use of "*a priori*" and "necessary" should be avoided: it leads only to confusion, and there is already a good term for it, namely Carnap's "L-determinate".[3] Using this term, we can say that there is no formal argument for supposing that an L-determinate proposition cannot entail a proposition which is not L-determinate.

Let us now return to the questions: Does (1) entail (3)? Does (2) entail (3)?

So far we have always used "entails" to mean strictly implies; and if we continue to do so, then trivially (1) entails (3), and also

---

[1] Already in the late 1940s and early 1950s, when the view that a contingent proposition cannot entail a necessary proposition was quite common, I argued against it. Cf. my paper "Entailment and Necessary Propositions" in M. Black (ed.) *Philosophical Analysis* (Ithaca, New York, 1950). Cf. also the entry "Lewy on entailment" in G. E. Moore's *Commonplace Book 1919–1953* (London, 1962).

[2] Wisdom used it in a discussion at the Cambridge Moral Science Club in 1952.

[3] R. Carnap, *Introduction to Semantics* (Cambridge, Mass., 1942), p. 94. "L-determinate" is of course an abbreviation for "logically determinate".

(2) entails (3) – for (3) is necessary, and is thus entailed by any proposition whatever.

Wisdom and many others (including myself) wished to distinguish between entailment and strict implication; but whether we can do so at all, and if so how, is a complex and difficult problem which I will discuss in detail in Chapters 9 and 10. Until then I wish to continue to identify entailment with strict implication,[1] and wish to consider the relationship between (1) and (3) and that between (2) and (3) without relying on a distinction between "entails" and "strictly implies".

But how can we do so? I think we must now reinterpret what Wisdom means by saying that (3) "makes no factual claims" which (1) does not make or which (2) does not make. In the present Chapter I will only do so in relation to the two questions: "Does (3) make no factual claims which (1) does not make?" and "Does (3) make no factual claims which (2) does not make?". In Chapter 8 I will try to generalize this discussion.

My reinterpretation is as follows.

(3) makes no factual claims which (1) does not make if and only if any proposition of the form:

    (A)   "‒‒‒" means the same as "..."

strictly implies the corresponding proposition of the form:

    (B)   The concept of being a ‒‒‒ is identical with the concept of being a...,

where the dashes in (A) and (B) are to be replaced by the same word and the dots by same expression.

And:

(3) makes no factual claims which (2) does not make if and only if any proposition of the form:

    (A′)   "‒‒‒" means...

strictly implies the corresponding proposition of the form:

    (B)   The concept of being a ‒‒‒ is identical with the concept of being a...

(subject to an analogous condition about the dashes and dots).

On this interpretation of what Wisdom may have meant, he was wrong.[2]

---

[1] I shall in general use the term "strictly implies"; but sometimes, for stylistic reasons, I shall use "entails" as a synonym.

[2] There is obviously no need to consider explicitly analogous interpretations for "(2) makes no factual claims which (1) doesn't make" and "(1) makes no factua

For the sake of brevity let me give the following definitions:

(1) ⇒ (3) if and only if (3) makes no factual claims which (1) does not make (as defined above);

and:

(2) ⇒ (3) if and only if (3) makes no factual claims which (2) does not make (as defined above).

Let us read "(1) ⇒ (3)" as "(1) justifies (3)", and "(2) ⇒ (3)" as "(2) justifies (3)".

I will now show that neither (1) nor (2) justifies (3).

Consider:

(α)   "Vixen" means the same as "male fox";

(β)   The concept of being a vixen is identical with the concept of being a male fox.

It is clear that (1) justifies (3) only if (α) strictly implies (β) since (α) is of the form (A) and (β) is of the form (B). But (α) does *not* strictly imply (β). Why? Because (β) strictly implies:

(γ)   ∼ ◇ ∼ [(x) (x is a vixen ⊃ x is a male fox)].

Assuming that a proposition of the form "Necessarily..." is necessary if true, and impossible if false, (γ) is impossible. Hence, (β) is impossible; but (α) is contingent (though false); and a contingent proposition cannot strictly imply an impossible proposition. Hence, (α) does not strictly imply (β); hence (1) does not justify (3).

An analogous argument shows that (2) does not justify (3).

Consider:

(α′)   "Vixen" means male fox;

(β)   The concept of being a vixen is identical with the concept of being a male fox.

(α′) is contingent; (β) is impossible; hence (α′) ⊰̸ (β);[1] hence (2) does not justify (3).

What we are doing is this. It has been said that in some sense necessary propositions are "based on" or are "justified by" or "owe their truth to" linguistic conventions. But what did those people (i.e. the logical positivists) mean by this? Clearly, they didn't mean that necessary propositions are *strictly implied* by linguistic conventions. This is true but trivial: a necessary proposition is strictly implied by any proposition whatever. Hence, the positivists' theory, if interpreted in this way, would not establish any relationship

---

claims which (2) doesn't make": it is enough to have shown that (1) does not strictly imply (2) and that (2) does not strictly imply (1).

[1] "⊰̸" means "does not strictly imply".

between necessary propositions and linguistic conventions which doesn't hold between necessary propositions and any proposition whatever. Of course, the positivists did not explain what they meant by "linguistic conventions" either. But I take it that they meant propositions such as Wisdom's (1) or propositions such as Wisdom's (2) – which they confused with each other.

I have tried in this Chapter to reconstruct their theory that necessary propositions are justified by linguistic conventions in a way which would make it both clear and non-trivial. In this interpretation, however, the theory is false.

Next let us consider the following proposition:

(4)   There is no vixen which is not a female fox.

Now Wisdom confuses *higher-order* necessary propositions, such as modal propositions and propositions giving analyses of concepts, with propositions such as (4), that is, with *first-order* necessary propositions. In particular he confuses (3) with "(x) (x is a vixen $\equiv$ x is a female fox)".[1]

So far I have assumed that all modal propositions are, if true, necessary. This, however, is a controversial matter which I shall discuss later in the present Chapter. What is *not* controversial is that propositions like (4) are necessary; and we must therefore consider whether *such* propositions are justified by either (1) or (2).

But before doing so, a brief digression will be in order. In the footnote on p. 463 (p. 63 in the book), to which I have already referred, Wisdom also makes the extraordinary assertion that it is characteristic of *necessary statements* – he in no way qualifies this – that "if [the hearer] denies them, the speaker says the hearer does not understand". So according to Wisdom *all* necessary statements are self-evident! There is simply no room for proof in logic or mathematics.

Moreover, he also says, in that very footnote, that logically necessary statements – again he in no way qualifies this – are *checked by the actual usage of language.* So *any* necessary statement in logic or mathematics is "checked by the actual usage of language"!

Let us return to (1), (2) and (4). We cannot, of course, interpret the assertion that (4) makes no factual claims which either (1) or

[1] Cf., e.g., "Metaphysics and Verification", p. 463 (p. 63 in *Philosophy and Psychoanalysis*), where he calls "Phoenixes are birds which renew themselves from their own ashes" an *analytic* statement.

(2) does not make, to mean that (1) strictly implies (4) and that (2) strictly implies (4). This would be true but trivial. So let us say:

(4) makes no factual claims which (1) doesn't make if and only if any proposition of the form:

(A) "———" means the same as "..."

strictly implies the corresponding proposition of the form:

(B′) There is no ——— which is not a...,

where the dashes in (A) and (B′) are to be replaced by the same word and the dots by the same expression.

Let us also say:

(4) makes no factual claims which (2) doesn't make if and only if any proposition of the form:

(A′) "———" means...

strictly implies the corresponding proposition of the form:

(B′) There is no ——— which is not a...

(subject to an analogous condition about the dashes and dots).

Also, let us use "(1) ⇒ (4)" and "(2) ⇒ (4)" in a way which should now be obvious without further explanation;[1] and let us read these formulae as "(1) justifies (4)" and "(2) justifies (4)", respectively.

I will now show that (1) does *not* justify (4).

Consider:[2]

(a) "Vixen" means the same as "male fox";

(b) Fido is a vixen;

(c) There is no vixen which is not a male fox.

I will show that (a) does not strictly imply (c): if so, then (1) does not justify (4).

Proof that (a) $\nrightarrow$ (c)

(I) If (a) $\dashv$ (c), then [(a) & (b)] $\dashv$ [(b) & (c)].

But   (II) [(b) & (c)] $\dashv$ Fido is a male fox.

And   (III) (b) $\dashv$ Fido is a female fox.

Hence (IV) [(b) & (c)] $\dashv$ Fido is a female fox.

Hence (V) [(b) & (c)] $\dashv$ Fido is a male fox *and* Fido is a female fox.

Call the consequent of (V), (Σ).

---

[1] In case this isn't obvious:

(1) ⇒ (4) if and only if (4) makes no factual claims which (1) doesn't make (as defined above);

(2) ⇒ (4) if and only if (4) makes no factual claims which (2) doesn't make (as defined above).

[2] In the arguments which follow I use the expression "male fox" to mean "fox of the male sex and *only* of that sex". I also use in this way the expression "lis płci męskiej".

(VI) (Σ) is logically impossible.

Hence (VII) $[(b) \& (c)]$ is logically impossible.

But (VIII) $[(a) \& (b)]$ is not logically impossible.

Hence (IX) $[(a) \& (b)] \twoheadrightarrow [(b) \& (c)]$.

Hence (X) $(a) \twoheadrightarrow (c)$.

It follows that (1) does not justify (4).

One way of seeing that the conjunction of (a) and (b) is logically possible is to translate the two sentences into Polish; we then get:

($a°$) "Vixen" znaczy to samo co "male fox";

($b°$) Fido jest lisicą.

It is then patent that the conjunction is logically possible.

We need this more complex proof in order to show that (a) does not strictly imply (c) because (c), unlike (β), is not itself a logically impossible proposition: if there were no vixens (c) would be true.

I have no doubt that this proof will strike some readers as fallacious. In fact it is perfectly in order. But before I discuss this I will give four further proofs that (a) does not strictly imply (c).

Second proof

Consider:

(a) "Vixen" means the same as "male fox";

(b) Fido is a vixen;

(c) There is no vixen which is not a male fox;

(d) There is no vixen which is not a female fox.

(I) If $(a) \twoheadrightarrow (c)$, then $[(a) \& (b) \& (d)] \twoheadrightarrow [(b) \& (d) \& (c)]$.

But (II) $[(b) \& (c)] \twoheadrightarrow$ Fido is a male fox.

And (III) $[(b) \& (d)] \twoheadrightarrow$ Fido is a female fox.

Hence (IV) $[(b) \& (c) \& (d)] \twoheadrightarrow$ Fido is a male fox *and* Fido is a female fox.

Call the consequent of (IV), (Σ).

Now (V) (Σ) is logically impossible.

Hence (VI) $[(b) \& (c) \& (d)]$ is logically impossible.

But (VII) $[(a) \& (b) \& (d)]$ is logically possible.

Hence (VIII) $[(a) \& (b) \& (d)] \twoheadrightarrow [(b) \& (d) \& (c)]$.

Hence (IX) $(a) \twoheadrightarrow (c)$.

Third proof

Take (a), (b), (c) and (d) again.

(I) $[(b) \& (d)] \twoheadrightarrow \sim (c)$.

Hence   (II)   If $(a) \prec (c)$, then $[(a) \mathbin{\&} (b) \mathbin{\&} (d)] \prec$
                   $[(c) \mathbin{\&} \sim (c)]$.
But   (III) $[(c) \mathbin{\&} \sim (c)]$ is logically impossible.
And   (IV) $[(a) \mathbin{\&} (b) \mathbin{\&} (d)]$ is logically possible.
Hence   (V) $[(a) \mathbin{\&} (b) \mathbin{\&} (d)] \not\prec [(c) \mathbin{\&} \sim (c)]$.
Hence   (VI) $(a) \not\prec (c)$.

Fourth proof

Take (a), (b), (c) and (d) again.

          (I) $[(b) \mathbin{\&} (d)] \prec \sim (c)$.
          (II) (d) is logically necessary.
Hence   (III) $(b) \prec \sim (c)$.
Hence   (IV)   If $(a) \prec (c)$, then $[(a) \mathbin{\&} (b)] \prec [(c) \mathbin{\&} \sim (c)]$.
But   (V) $[(c) \mathbin{\&} \sim (c)]$ is logically impossible.
And   (VI) $[(a) \mathbin{\&} (b)]$ is logically possible.
Hence   (VII) $[(a) \mathbin{\&} (b)] \not\prec [(c) \mathbin{\&} \sim (c)]$.
Hence   (VIII) $(a) \not\prec (c)$.

Fifth proof

Take (a), (b), (c) and (d) again.

          (I) (d) is logically necessary.
Hence   (II)   If $(a) \prec (c)$, then $(a) \prec [(c) \mathbin{\&} (d)]$.
But   (III) $[(c) \mathbin{\&} (d)] \prec (e)$ There are no vixens.
Hence   (IV)   If $(a) \prec (c)$, then $(a) \prec (e)$.
Hence   (V)   If $(a) \prec (c)$, then $\sim (e) \prec \sim (a)$.

That is, if $(a) \prec (c)$, then "There are vixens" $\prec \sim$ ("Vixen" means the same as "male fox").

This is a *reductio ad absurdum* of the claim that (a) strictly implies (c). For it is absurd to suppose that "There are vixens" strictly implies that the word "vixen" and the expression "male fox" do not mean the same.

We can now also show that (2) does not justify (4).
Consider:

    (a') "Vixen" means male fox;
    (b) Fido is a vixen;
    (c) There is no vixen which is not a male fox;
    (d) There is no vixen which is not a female fox.

(2) does not justify (4) unless $(a') \prec (c)$. But $(a') \not\prec (c)$.

Proof

          (I)   If $(a') \prec (c)$, then $[(a') \mathbin{\&} (b) \mathbin{\&} (d)] \prec$
                   $[(b) \mathbin{\&} (d) \mathbin{\&} (c)]$.

But (II) $[(b)$ & $(c)]$ ⊰ Fido is a male fox.

And (III) $[(b)$ & $(d)]$ ⊰ Fido is a female fox.

Hence (IV) $[(b)$ & (c) & $(d)]$ ⊰ (Σ) Fido is a male fox *and* Fido is a female fox.

But (V) (Σ) is logically impossible.

Hence (VI) $[(b)$ & (c) & $(d)]$ is logically impossible.

But (VII) $[(a')$ & (b) & $(d)]$ is logically possible.

Hence (VIII) $[(a')$ & (b) & $(d)]$ ⊰̸ $[(b)$ & (d) & $(c)]$.

Hence (IX) (a') ⊰̸ (c).

Hence (2) does not justify (4).

It is obvious that we can show in a similar way that neither (1) nor (2) justifies such other "first-order" necessary propositions as "There is no vixen which isn't female" and "There is no vixen which isn't a fox".

It should be noticed that if the above arguments are correct, we can show that neither (1) nor (2) justifies (3) in a different way from that given before, namely without assuming that (β) (see p. 52) is logically impossible. For clearly (β) strictly implies (4). Hence, since strict implication is transitive, if (α) ⊰ (β), then (α) ⊰ (4). But we have shown that (α) ⊰̸ (4). (The same applies, *mutatis mutandis*, to (α') and (4).)

I conclude that in the interpretation which we are now discussing the conventionalists' theory (one can also call it the reductionists' theory) is entirely false.

I realize however that my proofs will strike some readers as fallacious. Let me discuss what I think would be their objection, and let me do so in connexion with my *second* proof which is probably the most perspicuous. Consider again:

(*a*) "Vixen" means the same as "male fox";

(*b*) Fido is a vixen;

(*c*) There is no vixen which is not a male fox;

(*d*) There is no vixen which is not a female fox.

The objectors (i.e. the conventionalists) would no doubt deny that $[(a)$ & (b) & $(d)]$ is logically possible, i.e. they would reject step (VII) of the proof. They would say, I think, that this conjunction is logically *im*possible. That this is false is quite clear: we have seen that the conjunction of (*a*) and (*b*) is logically possible, and the addition of (*d*), which is itself logically necessary, cannot conceivably result in a conjunction which is *im*possible. But *why* do the conventionalists think that [(*a*) & (*b*) & (*d*)] is impossible? I believe the answer is as follows.

They think that (*a*) strictly implies that the *proposition* (*b*) is identical with the *proposition*

(*b'*)   Fido is a male fox;

and they also think that (*a*) strictly implies that the *proposition* (*d*) is identical with the *proposition*

(*d'*)   There is no male fox which is not a female fox.

Hence, they think that

$$[(a) \& (b) \& (d)] \equiv [(a) \& (b') \& (d')];^1$$

and since [(*a*) & (*b'*) & (*d'*)] is impossible (since [(*b'*) & (*d'*)] is so), they think that [(*a*) & (*b*) & (*d*)] is also impossible.

But they are entirely wrong: $(a) \twoheadrightarrow [(b) = (b')]$; and $(a) \twoheadrightarrow [(d) = (d')]$. All that is true is that if (*a*) were true (and if certain other conditions were also satisfied), then the *sentence* "Fido is a vixen" would express the proposition that Fido is a male fox. And this is *totally* different from supposing that $(a) \dashv 3 [(b) = (b')]$. And the same applies, *mutatis mutandis*, to (*d*) and (*d'*).

Hence conventionalism is due to the confusion between sentences and propositions. One might therefore say that the Conventionalist Error is based on the Nominalist Error.

All this is entirely clear if we translate (*a*), (*b*) and (*d*) into Polish:

(*a°*)   "Vixen" znaczy to samo co "male fox";

(*b°*)   Fido jest lisicą;

(*d°*)   Nie istnieje lisica która nie jest lisem płci żeńskiej.

It is *patently* absurd to suppose that

(*a°*) $\dashv 3$ [the *proposition* (*b°*) = the *proposition* (*b°'*) Fido jest lisem płci męskiej],

or that

(*a°*) $\dashv 3$ [the *proposition* (*d°*) = the *proposition* (*d°'*) Nie istnieje lis płci męskiej który nie jest lisem płci żeńskiej].

2

I have so far repeatedly assumed that propositions of the form "Necessarily..." are, if true, themselves necessary. I now wish to discuss this. In other words, I wish to discuss whether C. I. Lewis's

---

1 Or even that the respective conjunctions express the same proposition; but the weaker assumption will serve my purpose.

axiom C10 of the system S4 correctly reflects our pre-formal intuitions concerning logical necessity.[1]

Axiom C10 is:

$$\sim \Diamond \sim P \dashv \sim \Diamond \sim \sim \Diamond \sim P.$$

Lewis himself was unable to decide whether C10 is intuitively correct. (In fact his favourite system was S2.)

There is now substantial literature on the subject involving the so-called "possible worlds semantics" which I cannot here discuss. In any case, although I do not wish to minimize the value of this approach, it seems to me that the answer to our question must ultimately be based on more direct and purely philosophical considerations.

In this connexion I can do no more than repeat, albeit in an expanded form, arguments in favour of C10 which I gave a long time ago and which I do not think have been superseded.[2]

Consider:

(A) The proposition that there is no vixen which is not a fox is necessary.

(A) is true; but is it necessary?

First, what are the arguments *against* supposing so? Strawson's argument is as follows.[3] He says that entailment statements are contingent, and that necessary statements and their negations do not entail and are not entailed by anything. Strawson thinks (or rather, perhaps, thought at the time) that P entails Q if and only if (1) "$P \supset Q$" is necessary, (2) P is contingent, and (3) Q is contingent. I will discuss this later; what I wish to point out at present is that Strawson interprets (1) as being about the *expression* "$P \supset Q$". In our particular case, Strawson would say that (A) is about the *sentence* "There is no vixen which is not a fox".

The same view was expressed a little earlier by Reichenbach.[4] Reichenbach asks us to consider the two statements:

(1) $a \lor \sim a$

and

(2) statement (1) is a tautology,

[1] Cf. C. I. Lewis and C. H. Langford, *Symbolic Logic* (New York and London, 1932), esp. Appendix II.
[2] Cf. C. Lewy, "Entailment and Necessary Propositions" in M. Black (ed.), *Philosophical Analysis* (Ithaca, New York, 1950).
[3] P. F. Strawson, "Necessary Propositions and Entailment-Statements", *Mind*, vol. 57 (1948). See esp. pp. 184–6.
[4] H. Reichenbach, *Elements of Symbolic Logic* (New York, 1947).

and says (p. 186) that (2) "is an empirical statement about structural properties of the symbols occurring in (1)" (whatever that may mean).

The Reichenbach–Strawson view is incorrect. It is based on the confusion between (A) and

> (B)   The proposition expressed by the sentence "There is no vixen which is not a fox" is necessary.

(B) is contingent, but (A) and (B) are not identical since (A) does not strictly imply (B).

The view might stem from Wittgenstein, who thought that propositions of the form "$P \dashv Q$" are about symbolism, and are therefore contingent. (I am referring to his lectures on the Foundations of Mathematics given in Cambridge in 1939 which I attended.) Of course, Wittgenstein *never* said that propositions of the form "$P \supset Q$" are about symbolism: unlike Wisdom, he never confused, e.g., "Fido is a vixen $\supset$ Fido is a fox" with "Fido is a vixen $\dashv$ Fido is a fox".

I have two arguments *in favour* of supposing that (A) is itself a necessary proposition.

(1) How do we come to know that (A) is true? I think the answer is: by *reflecting* on the proposition – there is no need for an empirical inquiry. If so, it seems to follow that (A) is necessary. But – an objector might say – do we not need a *linguistic* inquiry, e.g. into how the words "vixen" and "fox" are used in English? And if we don't actually have to undertake such an inquiry, is this not because we are familiar with English? My reply to this would be as follows.

Compare (A) with

> (C)   There is no vixen which is not a fox.

Now (C) is agreed to be necessary. Is a linguistic inquiry needed to establish the truth of (C)? A positivist philosopher who thinks that a linguistic inquiry is needed to establish the truth of (A) must surely, by parity of reasoning, also think that such an inquiry is needed to establish the truth of (C) – or that if it is not *actually* needed this is because we are familiar with English. But if this is not inconsistent with the necessity of (C), why should it be inconsistent with the necessity of (A)?

(2) The above argument is epistemological: it involves reference to the concept of knowledge; and perhaps it might be questioned in ways which I have not considered. My second argument is purely logical, and I think it is conclusive.

If (A) is not necessary, then it is contingent, i.e. it *need not* have been necessarily true that there is no vixen which is not a fox. In other words, to suppose that (A) is not necessary is to suppose that a vixen which is not a fox, although not an *actual* possibility, is a *possible* possibility. And this is absurd.

Of course, the *sentence* "There is no vixen which isn't a fox" might have been used to express a contingent proposition: but this is no objection to the view that (A) is necessary. To suppose that it is, is once again to confuse propositions with sentences.

The view that there is *no answer* to the question whether (A) is necessary (von Wright,[1] possibly Lemmon[2]) can't be correct. For if it were, it would follow that that the *sentence* (A) expresses no definite proposition; but it does since there is no doubt at all that (A) is true! Von Wright's actual argument only shows that C10 is independent of Lewis's other axioms (which we knew already). Lemmon, on the other hand, is right in saying that if by "is necessary" we mean "is a tautology of the propositional calculus" then C10 must be rejected: the statement that something is a tautology of the propositional calculus is not itself a tautology of the propositional calculus. But this is irrelevant to our problem since it is clear that our pre-formal concept of logical necessity is not identical with that of being a tautology of the propositional calculus.

The view that true propositions of the form "Necessarily..." are not themselves necessary was also held by Moore in the paper on "External and Internal Relations". Moore says:

"P(x) *entails* Q(x)" is not *itself* a necessary proposition; but if "P(x) entails Q(x)" is *true*, then "P(x) $\supset$ Q(x)" is a necessary proposition.[3]

The second part of Moore's statement is undeniable; but he gives no reason for the first part. He repeats his claim at the beginning of the *Commonplace Book*, but again without giving any reasons. He says:

A proposition which asserts necessity, asserts of some other pro-

G. H. von Wright, "Interpretations of Modal Logic", *Mind*, vol. 61 (1952). Reprinted in G. H. von Wright, *Logical Studies* (London, 1957).
[2] E. J. Lemmon, "Is There Only One Correct System of Modal Logic?", *Aristotelian Soc. Suppl. Vol.* 33 (1959).
[3] *Philosophical Studies*, p. 302. This sentence does not occur in the *PAS* version. I have slightly altered Moore's symbolism.

position that it is necessary. Thus "Every right angle *must* be an angle" is not itself necessary.[1]

A clue to what may, I think, have been at the back of his mind is given in a much later entry in the *Commonplace Book* (p. 317). This entry is not entirely clear, but I believe the main point is as follows. Moore says that

$$P \mathbin{\&} (P \supset Q) \mathbin{\&} \sim Q$$

is of course a contradiction; but asks whether a man who says that this is *not* a contradiction, is contradicting himself. And he says that such a man is saying something which is *necessarily false*, "but that doesn't seem to be the same thing".

It is clear from this that although Moore was in the end prepared to agree that, e.g., the negation of the proposition "Necessarily, there is no vixen which isn't a fox" is *necessarily false*, and hence that the proposition itself is necessarily true, he wished to distinguish between saying that something is necessarily false and that it is a contradiction.

Can we elucidate this? Logicians often assume that *every* impossible proposition entails a contradiction, i.e. a proposition of the form "$P \mathbin{\&} \sim P$"; equivalently, they assume that *every* necessary proposition is entailed by a proposition of the form "$\sim (P \mathbin{\&} \sim P)$", i.e. of the form "$P \lor \sim P$".

For example, as we shall see later, C. I. Lewis produced what has been called an "independent proof" of his claim that an impossible proposition entails any proposition whatever. The proof is called "independent" in the sense that the principles used in it are all (it is alleged) intuitively acceptable and do not depend on Lewis's definition of "entails". (For he has defined "P entails Q" as "$\sim \Diamond (P \mathbin{\&} \sim Q)$", and from this his claim follows immediately.) But even if his proof is valid, it is only a proof that a proposition of the form "$P \mathbin{\&} \sim P$" entails any proposition whatever. Yet it is often thought that it is a proof that *any* impossible proposition entails anything whatever – and this relies on the unproved and unstated assumption that any impossible proposition entails a proposition of the form "$P \mathbin{\&} \sim P$". Thus there is a hiatus between Lewis's definition of "entails" and what his "independent" proof, if valid, really shows.

I do not know how one can prove the above assumption, and in

---

[1] G. E. Moore, *Commonplace Book 1919–1953* (London, 1962), p. 5.

fact I doubt whether it is true – unless, of course, one identifies entailment with strict implication. For how can one give an "independent" proof that, e.g., "$\Diamond (P \& \sim P)$", which is itself logically impossible, entails something of the form "$(P \& \sim P)$"? (If $\sim \Diamond \sim P \dashv \sim \Diamond \sim \sim \Diamond \sim P$, then

(1)　$\sim \Diamond \sim [\sim (P \& \sim P)]$

is itself necessary; hence its negation:

(2)　$\Diamond (P \& \sim P)$

is impossible.)

If I am right in this, then the position seems to be as follows. Lewis's unstated and unproved assumption is in fact based on the assumption that C10 is unacceptable. (Perhaps this is why Lewis didn't like S4 – but so far as I know, he nowhere discusses the relation between S4 and his unstated assumption.) So that if C10 is accepted, the gap between Lewis's proof and what is required by his definition of entailment cannot be bridged.

In this case Moore would be right in thinking that "necessarily false" does not mean the same as "self-contradictory"; but this, far from being a reason for *denying* that true propositions of the form "Necessarily..." are themselves necessary, presupposes that they are.

Moreover, if true propositions of that form are themselves necessary, then an important part of Wittgenstein's philosophy of logic in the *Tractatus* is wrong. He identifies propositions of logic with tautologies (6.1) in his technical sense (4.46), and says (5.525): "The certainty, possibility, or impossibility of a situation is not expressed by a proposition, but by an expression's being a tautology, a proposition with sense, or a contradiction".[1] (Cf. also 4.464.) Actually he should have said in 5.525 "necessity" (*Notwendigkeit*), not "certainty" (*Gewissheit*). But at that time he thought that only necessary propositions are certain – contingent propositions, he thought, can only be more or less probable.

But doesn't "It is necessary that $P \supset P$"[2] express the necessity of a situation? Clearly it does. There is no *tautology* which expresses this necessity, but there is a necessary proposition which expresses it – the modal proposition just given.

---

[1] L. Wittgenstein, *Tractatus Logico-Philosophicus* (London, 1922). I follow the translation by D. F. Pears and B. F. McGuinness (London, 1961).

[2] Strictly speaking, "For every P, it is necessary that $P \supset P$". But we can disregard this here.

I have now discussed C10. Analogous arguments can be given in favour of Lewis's axiom C11:

$$\Diamond\, P \rightarrow\!3 \sim \Diamond \sim \Diamond\, P.$$

This axiom forms a part of the System S5 (which includes S4). I think that S5 correctly reflects our pre-formal concepts of logical necessity and logical possibility.

3

This is a suitable place to make some additional points arising out of our preceding discussions.

1. The so-called "translation device" or "translation argument" is clearly right when applied to *transparent* contexts, and also when quotation is involved if the quotation in question can be treated in the Tarski–Carnap–Quine way as syntactically simple (e.g. as in the sentence "The English word "dog" has three letters"). It can only be subject to even *prima facie* (though mistaken) doubt when applied to *opaque* contexts (other than those which involve only quotation of the kind mentioned above).

2. Dummett's recent criticism of the translation device is entirely incorrect.[1] He says that there is no ground for presumption that the practical canons of apt translation always require strict synonymity. But this criticism reveals a misunderstanding of the *purpose* of the translation device, and in fact Dummett is giving away his case altogether without seeing that he is doing so. For the device is merely a device for showing that α and β are *not* synonymous (in Dummett's terminology, "not strictly synonymous"[2]) when it has been alleged that they are; so the fact that for some purposes translation need not preserve strict synonymity is simply irrelevant. Let me put the matter in a slightly different way. Suppose, for instance, that I argue as follows: "α and β are not synonymous: for if we translate α and β into Latin we get α' and β' respectively, and it is obvious that α' and β' are not synonymous". To this Dummett replies: "If you require of a correct translation that it should preserve synonymity, then α' is a correct translation of α, and β' of β; but there is a sense of "correct translation" in which this is *not* required". Hence, Dummett has already granted that α

---

[1] M. Dummett, *Frege: Philosophy of Language* (London, 1973), p. 372.
[2] In what follows I use "synonymous" to mean what Dummett means by "strictly synonymous".

and β are not synonymous. If so, then of course the translation device is no longer required. Dummett has granted me my conclusion![1]

I should add that in this work I have also used the translation device in a slightly different way, namely to show that one proposition, say P, does not entail another, say Q (when it has been thought by some philosophers that it did); and I have done so by showing that if the sentences expressing P and Q are translated into Latin or Polish, we get two sentences α and β such that it is obvious that the proposition expressed by α does not entail the proposition expressed by β. This, however, does not affect my criticism of Dummett: there may be a sense of "correct translation" in which α and β are not correct translations of the respective English sentences; but as long as it is agreed that α is synonymous with the one and β with the other and that the proposition expressed by α does not entail the proposition expressed by β, my argument goes through.

To sum up the matter. The sense of "correct translation" which I am using is that which *does* require strict synonymity. Hence, to point out that there is a sense of "correct translation" which does *not* require it, is just irrelevant.

Geach's treatment of the matter seems to me to be equally irrelevant. He says:

"God said 'Let there be light'" does not mean that God used English, and only a philosopher would argue that this is a mistranslation unless the original consisted of a quoted English sentence standing in a Hebrew context.[2]

Indeed, "God said "Let there be light"" does not entail that

---

[1] To put the matter more formally. It is obvious that if α' is not synonymous with β', then α is not synonymous with β or α is not synonymous with α' or β is not synonymous with β'. Dummett implicitly grants that α' is not synonymous with β'; that α is synonymous with α'; and that β is synonymous with β'. He must therefore grant that α is not synonymous with β.

Moreover, my criticism of Dummett *must* be right: for it would be *patently* absurd to claim that it is only in that sense (or those senses) of "correct translation" in which a correct translation need *not* be synonymity-preserving that, e.g., my sentences (1a) and (2a) in Chapter 1 are correct translations into Latin of Wisdom's sentences (1) and (2) respectively. I think it is clear that Dummett is not making this absurd claim.

[2] P. T. Geach, "The Identity of Propositions", *Księga Pamiątkowa ku czci Tadeusza Kotarbińskiego* (Warsaw, 1967). Reprinted in P. T. Geach, *Logic Matters* (Oxford, 1972), p. 167.

God used English; but "God said "Let there be light"" does not mean "God uttered the words "Let there be light"".

And has Geach overlooked the fact that if I translated:

  (*a*) Churchill uttered the words "We shall never surrender"
into Polish by:

  (*b*) Churchill wymówił słowa "My się nigdy nie poddamy",
I should be turning a truth into a falsehood?

I do not deny that for *some purposes* it would be legitimate to translate (*a*) by (*b*); but in this sense of "translation", translation need not be truth-preserving. It is entirely clear that there is *another* sense of "translation" in which translation *must* be truth-preserving; and it ought to be equally clear that it is this latter sense that is involved in the translation argument.

3. I have pointed out that Wisdom confuses modal and other higher-order necessary propositions with first-order necessary propositions. In particular, he confuses his (3) with:

  (3′)   (*x*) (*x* is a vixen ≡ *x* is a female fox).

I wish now to point out explicitly that this is a result of another and more fundamental confusion: he seems unaware of the distinction between transparent contexts and opaque contexts, and attributes to *all* sentences expressing necessary propositions features which in fact are only possessed by those of them that are opaque. (I.e. those sentences which express modal propositions, propositions giving analyses of concepts, etc.)

Moreover, it is the same fundamental failure to distinguish between transparent contexts and opaque contexts which vitiates the rest of his discussion, too.[1] For let us take, instead of his

  (α)   She is chic,
  (A)   Her lips are red.

(What is true of the former, must be true of the latter.) If (α) can be "turned into" a statement about words:

  (α′)   She is what the French call "chic",

if and only if (α′) is so used that we say that a man understands it only if he understands not merely the expression "what the French call "chic"" but also understands the word "chic", then (A) can also be "turned into" a statement about words:

  (A′)   Her lips are what the English call "red",

---

[1] See *Philosophy and Psycho-analysis*, p. 63 and the footnote on that page (quoted at the beginning of Chapter 1).

if and only if (A′) is so used that we say that a man understands it only if he understands not merely the expression "what the English call "red"" but also understands the word "red". Hence, *all* statements can be "turned into" statements about words if and only if, etc. So that Wisdom has *not* avoided the still pretty extreme paradox of supposing that all statements are *partly* verbal. The whole theory is therefore absurd. And one of the main sources of this absurd theory is Wisdom's failure to notice the crucial distinction between

(A)   Her lips have the characteristic of being red (i.e. are red)

and

(B)   John believes that her lips are red.

(A) is transparent whilst (B) is opaque. It is absurd to suppose that (A) can be "turned into" a statement about words – it is only with respect to (B) that such a claim can be made with even the smallest plausibility (though in fact the claim is wrong – as is clear from our discussions).

But Wisdom does not see this; that is why he says (p. 62): "For every statement about abstract entities – propositions, characteristics – there is a verbal statement which makes the same factual claims". For *every* such statement! He does not even see that he has misconceived his problem. For the only kind of statement about abstract entities that is to be analysed, or explained, is the kind of statement exemplified by (B), that is, the kind of statement that is expressed by sentences which are opaque. It is hardly surprising in view of all this that his discussion is incoherent.

4. I think it is clear that there is *no* "use" of:

(Σ)   Smith uttered[1] the sentence "Africa is hot"

in which (Σ) cannot be understood unless the hearer understands the sentence "Africa is hot". And Wisdom does not even *attempt* to give any argument for supposing that there is. Moreover, even if there were such a use, what would be expressed by (Σ) in that use couldn't be logically equivalent to what is expressed by:

(Ω)   Smith asserted that Africa is hot.

For the proposition expressed by (Σ) would still have something about the English sentence "Africa is hot" as a logical consequence, whereas the proposition expressed by (Ω) does not.

Moreover, so far as the former point is concerned, Wisdom gives

---

[1] Wisdom should have added "assertively".

no further account of what that alleged use of (Σ) is. There is therefore no reason whatever for accepting his bare assertion that there is such a use. The alternative which seems clearly correct, but which Wisdom does not even mention, is that anybody who does know that the sentence "Africa is hot" means that Africa is hot, will be able to deduce from (Σ) *and* this extra piece of knowledge that Smith asserted that Africa is hot (at least in one sense of "assert" – that in which what a man asserts depends on the *ordinary* meaning of the words he utters assertively, and not on the meaning *he* attaches to them). But this is something totally different from what Wisdom wishes to maintain.

Wisdom has therefore done nothing to solve the problem of how to analyse opaque contexts.

5. Finally, I have not commented explicitly on what is perhaps the most curious claim in Wisdom's discussion, namely the claim that whilst (Σ) is logically equivalent to (Ω) if and only if the sentence (Σ) is used in his alleged way, (3) is logically equivalent to (1) when the sentence (1) is used in the Chinaman's (decoder's) way; and that *this* is the difference between statements which are *purely* verbal (i.e. (3) and – he thinks – *all* logically necessary statements) and statements which are not *purely* verbal such as (Ω).[1]

This claim is surely a final *reductio ad absurdum* of Wisdom's whole theory; but how could he have made it? I think we are now in a position to answer this. Wisdom fails to see that (Ω) and (3) are opaque whilst (α) and $(3')$ are transparent. He thinks his task is to give a reductionist analysis of all the four; and he then distinguishes (3) and $(3')$ on the one hand from (Ω) and (α) on the other by giving one analysis for (3) and $(3')$ – but the same for both because they are both necessary – and a different analysis for (Ω) and (α) – but the same for both because they are both contingent.

So (3) and $(3')$ – one opaque, the other transparent – get the same analysis! And (Ω) and (α) – one opaque, the other transparent – get the same analysis!

Thus Wisdom's theory is ultimately due not only to his failure to grasp the transparent–opaque distinction, but also to his confusing it with the contingent–necessary distinction.

[1] See his footnote, p. 63 (quoted in Chapter 1).

6

Meaning and reference: I

I will now discuss certain problems concerning meaning and reference. One way of doing so is by discussing the so-called "Paradox of Analysis".

I will present the Paradox in three forms. The word "entails", as used in this Chapter, may be understood to mean strictly implies.

Form I. Consider:

    (A)   The concept of being a vixen is identical with the concept of being a female fox;

    (B)   The concept of being a vixen is identical with the concept of being a vixen.

Now

    (1)   (A) does not entail anything about the *word* "vixen" or about the *expression* "female fox";

    (2)   If (A) and (1), then

    (3)   The proposition that the concept of being a vixen is identical with the concept of being a female fox is identical with the proposition that the concept of being a vixen is identical with the concept of being a vixen.[1]

But

    (4)   (3) is paradoxical.

That is, (3) is paradoxical in the sense of being counter-intuitive; i.e. I am using the word "paradoxical" in the same, entirely legitimate, sense in which Quine used it when he said, quite rightly, that it is paradoxical to suppose that, e.g., "The moon is round" entails that the English word "round" is meaningful. (See Chapter 2.)

Wisdom (like Wittgenstein, W. E. Johnson and the Frege of the

---

[1] I.e. the proposition (A) is identical with the proposition (B). For the sake o brevity I will sometimes use the phrase "the concept of a vixen" as a synonym for the phrase "the concept of being a vixen", and the phrase "the concept of a female fox" as a synonym for the phrase "the concept of being a female fox"; and I will similarly abbreviate other phrases of the form "the concept of being a ...".

Begriffsschrift) would of course deny (1). In this way the Paradox of Analysis would be avoided. We have already seen however that to suppose that (A) entails ""Vixen" means the same as "female fox"" is wrong.[1] Moreover, Wisdom himself thinks that (A) is a necessary proposition. If so, (1) cannot be false.

There is also the translation argument.

I. (A) is identical with
    (A') Pojęcie lisicy jest identyczne z pojęciem lisa płci żeńskiej;

II. (A') does *not* entail anything about the word "vixen" or the expression "female fox".

From (I) and (II), (1) follows immediately.

Are there any arguments for supposing (A) to be logically necessary? (Wisdom assumes that (A) is necessary, but gives no arguments.) I think there are.

Argument 1. If (A) is not necessary, then since it is true, it is contingent. But if (A) is contingent, then it is logically possible that (A) should have been false. But clearly this is *not* possible. (This may be concealed by confusing (A) with Wisdom's (1) which of course *is* contingent.)

Argument 2. How do we get to know the truth of (A)? By reflexion. That is to say, no empirical inquiry is needed.

In other words, there are the same reasons for supposing (A) to be necessary as for supposing that any true proposition of the form "Necessarily..." is necessary. (See Chapter 5.)

Let us now go back to the Paradox. Unless we accept (3), i.e. maintain that there is nothing paradoxical about (3), we must deny (A) or (2). To deny (A) means in effect that no proposition asserting identity of concepts is true, other than propositions such as (B). This I cannot accept: it just isn't true. Hence, we must deny (2). But before I discuss the matter further, let me give two other forms of the Paradox.

Form II. Consider:

(α) "Vixen" means female fox;

(β) "Vixen" means vixen;

(γ) The concept of being a vixen is identical with the concept of being a female fox.

---

[1] See Chapter 5. I am assuming here that if (1) is false, then (A) entails ""Vixen" means the same as "female fox"" ; but this is surely correct.

Now we proceed as follows.

(1) $[(\alpha) \ \& \ (\beta)]$ entails (γ);

(2) The occurrence of "female fox" in (α) does not entail anything about the *expression* "female fox", and the occurrence of "vixen" in (β) does not entail anything about the *word* "vixen";[1]

(3) If (γ) and (2), then

(4) The proposition that "vixen" means female fox is identical with the proposition that "vixen" means vixen.

But

(5) (4) is paradoxical.

This is enough for our main purpose; but we can continue as follows.

Hence   (6) Either (2) is false or (γ) is false or both;

but   (7) (2) is true;

hence   (8) (γ) is false;

but   (9) (β) is true;

hence   (10) (α) is false.

But   (11) (10) is paradoxical.

This extended version of Form II of the Paradox, i.e. the version including the last six steps, might be called the Paradox of Definition.

Form III. Consider:

(α') "Vixen" means vixen;

(β') "Female fox" means female fox;

(γ') "Vixen" means the same as "female fox";

(δ) The concept of being a vixen is identical with the concept of being a female fox;

(ϵ) The concept of being a vixen is identical with the concept of being a vixen.

Now

(1) $[(\alpha') \ \& \ (\beta') \ \& \ (\gamma')]$ entails (δ);

(2) (δ) does not entail anything about the *word* "vixen" or about the *expression* "female fox";

(3) If (δ) and (2), then

(4) The *proposition* (δ) is identical with the *proposition* (ϵ).

---

[1] Notice that in (2) the reference is to the occurrence of "vixen" in (β), *not* to the occurrence of ""vixen"".

But

    (5)   (4) is paradoxical.

So far Form III of the Paradox leads to the result which is the same as the result in Form I.

We can however continue Form III as follows.

Hence   (6)   Either (2) is false or (δ) is false or both;

but   (7)   (2) is true;

hence   (8)   (δ) is false;

but   (9)   (α') and (β') are true;

hence   (10) (γ') is false.

But   (11) (10) is paradoxical.

This extended version of Form III of the Paradox might be called the Paradox of Synonymity.

Historical remarks. It will be obvious that Forms II and III of the Paradox are extracted, with changes and adaptations, from Moore's very complicated and rather confusing paper "Russell's 'Theory of Descriptions'".[1] Some of the changes are quite minor, but the following differences between Moore's exposition and my own should be mentioned. (*a*) Moore doesn't make it clear that "entails" may be understood to mean strictly implies – on the contrary, he says that in his paper he is using "entails" in a narrower sense (which he does not explain). (*b*) I have added the essential premiss (2) in each of the two forms. (Just as I have added the essential premiss (1) in the Standard Form of the Paradox, i.e. Form I.) As a result of this, what I have called the extended versions of the two forms are more complex than in Moore. (Moore does not distinguish between the simple and the extended versions.)

2

It is clear that one possible solution of the Paradox of Analysis is to deny premiss (1) in Form I and premiss (2) in Forms II and III. As I have already mentioned, this is in effect the *Begriffsschrift*–W. E. Johnson–Wittgenstein–Wisdom solution.[2] I think however that

---

[1] In P. A. Schilpp (ed.), *The Philosophy of Bertrand Russell* (Evanston and Chicago, 1944). Moore's paper is reprinted in G. E. Moore, *Philosophical Papers* (London, 1959); see pp. 177ff.

[2] So far as Wittgenstein is concerned, cf. Moore's paper on Wittgenstein's lectures in 1930–33 in *Mind*, vols. 63 (1954) and 64 (1955). (Reprinted in Moore's *Philosophical Papers*.) I may add that Wittgenstein must have held this view, at least by implication, as late as 1939. For as I have already said, he then maintained that

I have said enough in the course of this work to show that this solution is unacceptable.

Moore. Moore offers no complete solution of the Paradox.[1] But if we adapt his discussion to accord with my exposition of the Paradox, then his view is that in the case of Form I premiss (2) should be denied and in the case of Forms II and III premiss (3) should be denied. But he can give no justification for his view.

Carnap. I shall now discuss Carnap's solution.[2] As I will try to show, this solution is not at all satisfactory but is nevertheless of interest. It is roughly as follows.

Compare the following pairs:

$$2+5, \quad \text{II sum V};$$
$$\text{London is large}, \quad \text{London ist gross};$$
$$2+5 > 3, \quad \text{Gr [sum (II, V), III]}.$$

Each expression on the left-hand side is *intensionally isomorphic* with the corresponding expression on the right-hand side. Roughly, α and β are intensionally isomorphic if they are constructed in the same way out of elements which are L-equivalent down to the smallest units.[3] More roughly still, but perhaps more clearly, α and β are intensionally isomorphic when it is not merely the case that α and β are L-equivalent, but also that to each unit in the one there corresponds an L-equivalent unit in the other.[4]

Now compare the following pairs:

7 is greater than 3, the sum of 2 and 5 is greater than 3;
John is a brother, John is a male sibling.

Clearly, the two sentences in each pair are L-equivalent; but they are *not* intensionally isomorphic. Carnap now gives strict equivalence as his criterion of propositional identity and claims that, e.g., the proposition (A) is identical with the proposition (B), but

propositions of the form "$P \dashv Q$" are "about symbolism", and hence contingent. But clearly, (A) entails "The proposition "Fido is a vixen" is strictly equivalent to the proposition "Fido is a female fox""; so if this equivalence-proposition is contingent, (A) must also be contingent. And how could it be contingent unless it was "about symbolism"? For Johnson's views see W. E. Johnson, *Logic*, Pt. I (Cambridge, 1921), pp. 39ff. For Frege's early view see his *Begriffsschrift* (Halle, 1879). English trans. in J. van Heijenoort (ed.), *From Frege to Gödel* (Cambridge, Mass., 1967). [1] See *Philosophical Papers*, p. 183.

[2] See R. Carnap, *Meaning and Necessity* (Chicago, 1947), pp. 63–4.

[3] L-equivalence is the semantic correlate of strict equivalence; e.g. two sentences are L-equivalent if and only if the corresponding propositions are strictly equivalent. The term "L-equivalence" is of course an abbreviation for "logical equivalence".

[4] *Op. cit.* pp. 56–9.

that there is "an important difference between the meaning" of the *sentence* (A) and that of the *sentence* (B) in that the two sentences are not intensionally isomorphic.[1]

We can slightly amend Carnap's solution as follows. We can imagine him saying "If your criterion of propositional identity is strict equivalence, then (A) and (B) are identical; if, on the other hand, your criterion of propositional identity is intensional isomorphism of the respective sentences, then (A) and (B) are not identical". In the first case, he might continue, the conclusion (3) in Form I of the Paradox is fully acceptable, so the paradox is solved by denying (4). In the second case (4) is true, but (2) is false – the reason for the falsity of (2) being of course that (A) and (1) do not imply that the sentences (A) and (B) are intensionally isomorphic.

In my opinion, Carnap's solution does not solve the Paradox of Analysis at all. In fact, one might go so far as to say that Carnap fails to understand the intuitive basis of the paradox.

For consider:

(Σ) Fido is a vixen;
(Ω) Fido is a female fox.

Intuitively, one wishes to say that (Σ) and (Ω) are the same proposition. But from this it *seems* to follow that (A) and (B) are the same proposition: yet *this* is counter-intuitive. Now Carnap's solution gives us two possible criteria of propositional identity: L-equivalence and intensional isomorphism. But on the former criterion whilst (Σ) and (Ω) *are* identical, so are (A) and (B); on the latter criterion, on the other hand, (A) and (B) are *not* identical, but (Σ) and (Ω) are not identical either.[2]

A possible suggestion arising out of our discussion of Carnap. The paradox is insoluble in the sense that it shows that our intuitive, i.e. pre-formal, concept of propositional identity is inconsistent. For, on the one hand, we wish to accept the steps leading to (3); and, on the other hand, we *don't* wish to accept (3). This is patently inconsistent. All we can now do is to try to "reconstruct" that inconsistent concept.

[1] Carnap's example is actually not that of (A) and (B), but of "The concept of being a brother is identical with the concept of being a male sibling" and "The concept of being a brother is identical with the concept of being a brother". But I will continue to speak as if Carnap's examples were (A) and (B). Clearly, this will make no difference to the discussion of his theory.

[2] Cf. my review of Carnap's book in *Mind*, vol. 58 (1949).

I will try to show later that this suggestion is wrong. In the meantime, however, it should be noticed that even if the suggestion is right, it does not necessarily follow that the only, or the best, reconstruction would be on Carnapian lines. This would come to introducing *two* concepts of propositional identity, one based on strict equivalence, the other on intensional isomorphism. In the first case the conclusion of the paradox (i.e. (3) in Form I) would be acceptable; in the second case the conclusion would be clearly false. But in this case "Fido is a vixen" would be a different proposition from "Fido is a female fox".

Clearly, even if our intuitive concept of propositional identity is inconsistent, a rectification of the inconsistency on Carnapian lines seems very unsatisfactory.

We may also notice that if we wished to extend this treatment to identity of concepts, we should presumably have to say that there are two possible criteria here too, L-equivalence and intensional isomorphism; and that on the first criterion (A) is true, but on the second criterion (A) is false.[1]

Unless we took this course, we should be dissociating, very counter-intuitively, concept identity from propositional identity. And then the relation between concepts and propositions would become extremely obscure.

C. I. Lewis. Lewis does not discuss the Paradox of Analysis; but I think that a solution can be extracted from his paper on "The Modes of Meaning".[2]

Roughly speaking, he gives one criterion for the identity of *contingent* propositions, and a different criterion for the identity of

---

[1] Strictly speaking, L-equivalence and intensional isomorphism are semantic notions whilst propositional identity and concept identity are not. But this is now well known, and there is no point in making one's exposition excessively complicated to take account of this all the time.

In this connexion I should remind the reader that throughout this work I use numerals and letters sometimes as labels for propositions and sometimes as labels for sentences. I believe that this ambiguity is always resolved by the context. But in many places, where it is particularly important to avoid ambiguity, I prefix to the label the word "proposition" or the word "sentence", as the case requires.

I also think that it would be unnecessarily pedantic to use Quine's notation of corners.

Occasionally, for stylistic reasons, I use the word "statement"; I sometimes use it to mean proposition, and sometimes to mean sentence. I believe that this ambiguity, too, is always resolved by the context.

[2] C. I. Lewis, "The Modes of Meaning", *Philosophy and Phenomenological Research*, vol. 4 (1944).

necessary propositions. His criterion for the identity of contingent propositions is strict equivalence. His criterion for the identity of necessary propositions is much more complex.

He explains it as follows (p. 245):

> An expression in question is *elementary* in case it has no symbolized constituent, the intension of which is a constituent of the intension of the expression in question itself. Otherwise the expression in question is *complex*.

He then introduces the relation "being equivalent in analytic meaning" as follows (p. 246):

> Two expressions are *equivalent in analytic meaning*, (1) if at least one is elementary and they have the same intension, or (2) if, both being complex, they can be so analyzed into constituents that (a) for every constituent distinguished in either, there is a corresponding constituent in the other which has the same intension, (b) no constituent distinguished in either has zero-intension or universal intension, and (c) the order of corresponding constituents is the same in both, or can be made the same without alteration of the intension of either whole expression.

He concludes by saying (p. 246):

> We shall be in conformity with good usage if we say that two expressions are synonymous or equipollent, (1) if they have the same intension and that intension is neither zero nor universal, or (2) if, their intension being either zero or universal, they are equivalent in analytic meaning.

The application of all this to the Paradox of Analysis is fairly obvious: according to Lewis's theory (Σ) and (Ω) are the *same* proposition, but (A) and (B) are *different* propositions. For (Σ) and (Ω) are contingent and hence, since they are strictly equivalent, they are identical; but (A) and (B) are necessary; hence they are not identical unless the sentences (A) and (B) are equivalent in analytic meaning, and clearly they are not.

Thus Lewis escapes my objection to Carnap. And he avoids – and this was of course his main object – the highly counter-intuitive consequence of Carnap's criterion of propositional identity, namely the consequence that all necessary propositions are identical and that all impossible propositions are identical.[1]

In spite of this, Lewis's solution is totally mistaken.

Criticisms of Lewis's theory

1. Strict equivalence will not do as the criterion of identity even for contingent propositions.

Proof. Let us first make the following assumption which seems clearly true:

P is identical with Q if and only if Q is contained in P and P is contained in Q.[2]

We can now proceed as follows.

According to Lewis, if $P \equiv Q$, and P and Q are both contingent, then $P = Q$. But from this and our assumption, we get that if $P \equiv Q$, and P and Q are both contingent, then Q is contained in P and P is contained in Q. And from this it obviously follows that if $P \dashv3 Q$, and P and Q are both contingent, then Q is contained in P.

Now consider:

(1) The proposition expressed by the English sentence "There is no vixen which is not a fox" is the proposition that there is no vixen which is not a fox;

(2) The proposition that there is no vixen which is not a fox is necessary;

(3) The proposition expressed by the English sentence "There is no vixen which is not a fox" is necessary.

The conjunction of (1) and (2) strictly implies (3); (2) is necessary and can therefore be omitted; hence (1) strictly implies (3). But (1) and (3) are both contingent. It follows, on Lewis's theory, that (3) is contained in (1). But it clearly isn't: (1) does not contain the concept of necessity whilst (3) does contain it.

It follows that strict equivalence will not do as the criterion of identity even for contingent propositions.

Moreover, a conjunction one conjunct of which is necessary and

---

[1] In his treatment of propositional identity Carnap merely followed Wittgenstein, *Tractatus*, 5.141. See the next footnote.

[2] Cf. *Tractatus*, 5.122: "If p follows from q, the sense of 'p' is contained in the sense of 'q'." 5.141: "If p follows from q and q from p, then they are one and the same proposition."

(It is clear that by "follows from" Wittgenstein means "is strictly implied by".) I shall symbolize "P is identical with Q" by "$P = Q$".

the other contingent is itself contingent. Hence, on Lewis's criterion, the following propositions are identical:

London is the capital of England and there is nothing which is red and is not coloured;

London is the capital of England, and there is no vixen which is not a fox.

This is surely counter-intuitive. In fact, it is nearly, if not quite, as counter-intuitive as the view that "There is nothing which is red and is not coloured" is the same proposition as "There is no vixen which is not a fox" – a view which Lewis himself found counter-intuitive. In fact, his main purpose in introducing the concept of equivalence in analytic meaning was to exclude this kind of case!

2. Compare:

$$1 + 1 = 3;$$
$$\sim \sim (1 + 1 = 3);$$

London is larger than Cambridge;

$$\sim \sim (\text{London is larger than Cambridge}).$$

According to Lewis, the last two propositions are identical, but the first two propositions are not identical. This seems to me counter-intuitive. Moreover, there is no reason to suppose that "is identical with" means one thing when it is applied to contingent propositions, and an entirely different thing when it is applied to logically impossible propositions. And if it does mean different things in the two kinds of case, it follows that when we don't know whether a proposition is contingent or impossible (and there is of course no effective decision procedure for determining when a sentence expresses an impossible proposition), the phrase "the proposition that..." has no definite sense at all.

3. Lewis's theory does *not* solve the Paradox of Analysis in Form II. This is so because according to Lewis whilst (A) and (B), in Form I of the Paradox, are *not* identical, (α) and (β), in Form II of the Paradox, *are* identical: for (α) and (β) are strictly equivalent and they are both contingent.

This in itself shows that Lewis's ideas are badly confused, and that he has failed to grasp the real source of the Paradox of Analysis. It is therefore decisive against Lewis, and also provides one reason why it is important to formulate the Paradox in Form II.

But let me point out some further consequences of Lewis's theory.

4. Consider:

    (*a*)   Fido is a vixen $\supset$ Fido is a fox;

    (*b*)   Fido is a female fox $\supset$ Fido is a fox.

On Lewis's theory (*a*) is not identical with (*b*). This cannot be accepted. The sentences (*a*) and (*b*) are purely truth-functional; the word "vixen" is synonymous, on Lewis's criterion of synonymity, with the expression "female fox"; yet, according to him, (*a*) and (*b*) are different propositions. In other words, according to Lewis the substitution of synonym for synonym in a truth-functional sentence may alter the meaning of the sentence. And this is absurd.

5. We should notice that Lewis's theory has also the following consequence.

Consider (*c*) "This has shape" and (*d*) "This has size". On Lewis's theory these are one and the same proposition! Surely there is something *very* wrong with a theory which makes (*c*) and (*d*) the *same* proposition, but (*a*) and (*b*) *different* propositions.

In fact, Lewis's theory makes it impossible to distinguish between the meanings of any two words or expressions which are such that (1) they necessarily apply to the same things, and (2) neither of them necessarily applies to everything and neither of them necessarily applies to nothing. This is unacceptable as the example of "shape" and "size" shows. And that "shape" and "size" *don't* mean the same is indisputable – there are things which are of the same shape but of different size, and there are things which are of the same size but of different shape. Thus a philosopher who says that "shape" and "size" mean the same is saying something which is *patently* false.

It is already clear from §§ 1, 2, 3 and 4 – and it will become even clearer later – that Lewis has restricted the substitutivity principle for synonyms in a highly artificial and counter-intuitive manner. He rightly thought that his restriction will get rid of the *Tractatus*–Carnap view that all necessary propositions are identical and that all impossible propositions are identical; but he quite failed to see that it would itself have entirely unacceptable consequences.

6. Lewis's "equivalence in analytic meaning" is not transitive, and hence it is not an equivalence relation. (It therefore differs from Carnap's intensional isomorphism which presumably *is* transitive.) This can be shown as follows. Let us symbolize Lewis's "equi-

valence in analytic meaning" by "$\approx$". Now consider these three propositions:

"Male sibling" $\approx$ "Brother";

"Brother" $\approx$ "Male being related to others as the child of the same parents";[1]

"Male sibling" $\approx$ "Male being related to others as the child of the same parents".

According to Lewis's theory, the first two propositions are true but the third is false. The third is false since the expressions which occur on each side of the equivalence sign in the third sentence are both complex; hence, the case falls under condition (2) in Lewis's explanation of equivalence in analytic meaning (see p. 76); but there is no constituent in the expression on the left-hand side which has the same intension as "child" or "parents" both of which occur in the expression on the right-hand side.

It follows from this taken alone that Lewis's "equivalence in analytic meaning" does not capture, or give an acceptable reconstruction of, the intuitive relation of synonymity: for obviously this is transitive.

I conclude (1) that Lewis has failed to solve the Paradox of Analysis, and (2) that he has entirely failed to produce a satisfactory analysis, or reconstruction, of synonymity.[2]

Frege. Frege does not explicitly discuss the Paradox of Analysis. But various things that he says in "Sinn und Bedeutung"[3] about identity-statements in general can be applied to the Paradox.[4]

For reasons which will become clear later, the best way to begin is by considering Form II of the Paradox, especially the two sentences:

(α)   "Vixen" means female fox;

(β)   "Vixen" means vixen.

If I understand Frege correctly, he would say that in the sentence (α) the expression "female fox" is used obliquely, and that in the sentence (β) the word "vixen" is used obliquely.[5] That is to say, in

---

[1] Adapted slightly from the *Oxford English Dictionary.*

[2] I will make further comments on Lewis's theory of meaning later. See Chapter 7.

[3] G. Frege, "Ueber Sinn und Bedeutung", *Z. für Philosophie und philosophische Kritik*, vol. 100 (1892). English trans. by M. Black in P. Geach and M. Black (eds.), *Translations from the Philosophical Writings of Gottlob Frege* (Oxford, 1952).

[4] This was pointed out for the first time by Alonzo Church in *Journal of Symbolic Logic*, vol. 11 (1946), pp. 132–3.

[5] I refer of course to the occurrence of the word "vixen" in (β), not to the occurrence of the expression ""vixen"".

(α) the reference[1] of the expression "female fox" is the *concept* of being a female fox, and *not* the class of female foxes; and in (β) the reference of the word "vixen" is the *concept* of being a vixen, and *not* the class of vixens.

Now the concept of being a vixen is identical with the concept of being a female fox; that is, the *ordinary* sense of the word "vixen" is the same as the *ordinary* sense of the expression "female fox". But their oblique senses are different. This is why step (3) in Form II of the Paradox of Analysis is invalid. And let us say for the moment that for the same reason step (2) in Form I and step (3) in Form III are invalid. (But the last point will be discussed at length presently.)

Thus Frege's theory of ordinary and oblique senses and references appears *prima facie* to provide a solution of the Paradox. It is on the same lines as Moore's solution in that the steps in the derivation of the Paradox that are declared to be invalid are the same in both; but it goes much beyond Moore's solution: for it explains, or purports to explain, precisely that which Moore was unable to explain, namely *why* the steps in question are invalid. That is, Moore did not have a *theory* of meaning on which the solution of the Paradox could be based.

We must now however discuss Frege's theory in detail.

Let us begin by asking: What *is* the oblique sense of the word "vixen"? I think that Frege's view is that the oblique sense of the word "vixen" is the ordinary sense of the words (*a*) "the concept of being a vixen", and that the oblique sense of the expression "female fox" is the ordinary sense of the words (*b*) "the concept of being a female fox".[2] Frege must therefore hold that the ordinary sense of (*a*) is different from the ordinary sense of (*b*). How can this be done?

This seems to me to be a very complex and difficult matter which I will try to discuss as well as I can.

In the first instance I will approach it rather indirectly.

---

[1] I shall generally use "reference" as the translation of Frege's "Bedeutung" (as was done by Max Black and is now the usual practice); but occasionally I shall translate it by "denotation", as was done by Church. I use "sense" as the translation of Frege's "Sinn"; and I translate "ungerade" as "oblique", and "gewöhnliche" as "ordinary".

[2] See "Ueber Sinn und Bedeutung", p. 37. (Pp. 66–7 in P. Geach and M. Black (eds.), *Translations from the Philosophical Writings of Gottlob Frege*.)

My use of the word "concept" is meant of course to correspond to Frege's use of "Sinn", *not* to his use of "Begriff".

I believe that this interpretation of Frege is right.

7

Meaning and reference: II

Let us ask the following question. What does really happen when a man (1) is able to apply correctly the word "vixen", (2) is able to apply correctly the expression "female fox", (3) is able to understand the question "What is the analysis of the concept of being a vixen?", and (4) *cannot* give a correct answer to this question?

I think the position is as follows. Such a man has the concept of being a vixen (and hence he has the concept of being a female fox); he has the concept "the concept of being a vixen"; he has the concept "the concept of being a female fox"; but he doesn't know that these last two concepts are concepts of the *same* concept. And he will acquire this knowledge by being told "The concept of being a vixen is identical with the concept of being a female fox".

Now let us suppose that a man satisfies conditions (1), (3) and (4), but does *not* satisfy condition (2); and let us also suppose (5) that he is unable to apply correctly *any* expression (in any language) which defines the word "vixen". Such a man will *not* have the concept "the concept of being a female fox"; but he *will* have the concept of being a female fox – this follows from the fact that he satisfies condition (1) – since he will then have the concept of being a vixen, and this concept is identical with the concept of being a female fox.

But if so, then it follows immediately that the concept of being a female fox is different from the concept "the concept of being a female fox"; that is, it follows immediately that we *must* distinguish between concepts and concepts *of* concepts.

Moreover, a man who satisfies conditions (1), (3), (4) and (5), but does *not* satisfy condition (2), will have the concept "the concept of being a vixen", but will *not* have the concept "the concept of being a female fox". Hence, we must also distinguish between the senses of the last two expressions. We must distinguish, in other words, between *different* concepts of the *same* concept.

Now in the *second* case the man in question will not be able to give a correct analysis of the concept of being a vixen because he will not have the concept "the concept of being a female fox", and also – this follows from (5) – he will have *no* concept which is a concept of the concept of being a vixen *other than* the concept "the concept of being a vixen".

Thus, and this is the third conclusion we may draw from the present discussion, we must distinguish *two quite different cases* when a man who is able to apply the word "vixen" correctly and who has the concept "the concept of being a vixen", cannot give a correct answer to the question "What is the analysis of the concept of being a vixen?"[1]

To make all this clearer let us consider the following situation.

Let us imagine a community of people who (1) use the word "mother" exactly as we do – apply it to mothers and *only* to mothers; (2) have no word or expression which means parent; (3) have no word or expression which means father; and (4) do not distinguish in any way between fathers and those males who are not fathers.

So far as I can see, the above set of conditions is consistent; and if so, then it follows that it is logically possible to have the concept of a mother, and hence the concept of a parent, without having a name for the latter concept.[2] That is, without having the word "parent" or another word or expression (in any language) which means parent. For there is no reason whatever for denying that the word "mother", as those people use it, means female parent.

It follows (1) that it is logically possible to have the concept of a female parent without having the concept "the concept of a parent", and hence without having the concept "the concept of a female

---

[1] It may be worth mentioning that Moore never made this important distinction. Cf. "A Defence of Common Sense", *Contemporary British Philosophy*, 2nd Ser. (London, 1925); reprinted in his *Philosophical Papers*. All that Moore tells us, in a celebrated passage (*Phil. Papers*, p. 37), is that one must not confuse the question whether we understand a sentence's meaning with the entirely different question whether we *know what it means* in the sense that we are able to *give a correct analysis* of its meaning. In the *Lectures on Philosophy* (London, 1966) he speaks of the first sense of understanding as attaching to an expression its common meaning (p. 166). But in neither of these works, nor in his "Reply to my Critics" in the Schilpp volume, is there any hint of the distinction which I have tried to make above. (For the "Reply to my Critics" see P. A. Schilpp (ed.), *The Philosophy of G. E. Moore* (Evanston and Chicago, 1942).)

[2] I will now generally abbreviate "the concept of being a mother" to "the concept of a mother", "the concept of being a parent" to "the concept of a parent", etc.

parent". That is, I have again shown, I think this time conclusively, that we must distinguish between concepts and concepts *of* concepts.

It follows (2) that to have the concept of a parent is *not* the same as being able to use correctly the word "parent", or some word or expression in some language or other, which means parent. Wittgenstein once said, in a lecture, "A concept is a way of speaking". Our case shows that in at least one sense this is not true. Whether there is any sense in which it is, I don't know.

Moreover, we can add, without rendering our conditions inconsistent, that the people in question have the concept "the concept of being a mother". For clearly there is nothing in our conditions to exclude, e.g., their wondering whether the concept of a mother is analysable!

But if so, then it also follows (3) that it is logically possible to have the concept "the concept of a mother" without having the concept "the concept of a female parent". That is, I have again shown, I think this time conclusively, that we must distinguish between *different* concepts of the *same* concept.

Further, we should notice that if in our imaginary case someone introduced the concept "the concept of a female parent", and said that the concept of a mother is identical with the concept of a female parent, this would be true and at the same time could perfectly rightly be said to be a discovery.

There are a number of further points which I wish to make in this connexion.

1. I think that many cases (perhaps most cases) which are of philosophical interest are those in which we can't tell what a word means, in the sense of being unable to give a correct analysis of its meaning, because although the word expresses a compound concept, we have no name for one (or more) of its constituent concepts.

That is to say, I think that many cases (perhaps most cases) which are of philosophical interest are cases of the *second* kind which I distinguished at the beginning of this Chapter, and not those of the *first* kind.

I think that Cantor's analysis of the concept of equinumerosity is an example of an analysis of the second kind.[1]

---

[1] G. Cantor, *Gesammelte Abhandlungen mathematischen und philosophischen Inhalts* (Berlin, 1932). See also B. Russell, *The Principles of Mathematics* (Cambridge,

"The class of husbands has the same number of members as the class of wives" means that there is a one–one relation of which the former class is the domain and the latter class the converse domain.

Must a man who has the concept of equinumerosity have the concepts of domain, converse domain and one–one relation? I think he must; and certainly he must if the above is what "equi-numerous" *means*. But surely he need not have any names for these concepts.

People sometimes say that Cantor's definition is not really an analysis, but involves a rectification of an inconsistency. But in my opinion no convincing reasons have been given for saying this.

2. We should notice that the case of our imaginary community also shows that a concept is *not* a "recognitional capacity". For members of that community do have the concept of a parent, but they do *not* distinguish between parents and non-parents. For they do not distinguish between fathers and *male* non-fathers; hence they do not distinguish between fathers and non-fathers; and hence they do not distinguish between parents and non-parents.

3. We should also notice that our case shows quite conclusively that there *is* a distinction between sense and reference. For the reference of the phrase "the concept of a mother" is the same as the reference of the phrase "the concept of a female parent". Yet the senses of the two phrases, that is, the concepts expressed by the two phrases, *must* be different: for our case shows that it is logically possible to have the first concept without having the second.

Finally, our case also shows that there is a distinction between concept and intension in Carnap's sense.[1] For the intension of the first phrase, in Carnap's sense of "intension", is the same as the intension of the second phrase.

Of course, in order to show that there is a distinction between sense and reference it is enough to point out that one may have the concept of a man without having the concept of a featherless biped. Hence, however difficult it may be to give a satisfactory account of the distinction, its existence just *cannot* be denied. And the same is true of the distinction between sense and Carnap's intension.

1903), and A. N. Whitehead and B. Russell, *Principia Mathematica*, vol. 1 (Cambridge, 1910; 2nd edn, 1925).
[1] *Meaning and Necessity*, pp. 202–3. Cf. also §4 below.

It is common nowadays in philosophy to deny the existence of a distinction because it is difficult to give a satisfactory account of it. It seems to me that this kind of methodology is thoroughly unsound and can only lead to intellectual confusion.

4. We must notice, however, that "X knows what the word "mother" means", or "X understands the word "mother"", in the sense that X attaches to the word its common meaning, *cannot* mean "X is capable of applying the word "mother" correctly", if this in turn means "X is capable of applying the word "mother" to those and only those creatures that are *in fact* mothers". Why? Because all those and only those creatures that are in fact mothers are also *both* mothers *and* less than 200 years old. But if things changed, and X met a mother who was 250 years old and yet refused to apply to her the word "mother", this would show that he did *not* understand the word "mother".

That is to say, "understanding the word "mother"", or "knowing the meaning of the word "mother"" – even in the sense in which one can do so without being able to give "a correct analysis of its meaning" – can't be explained in terms which involve no reference to a *modal* notion, namely, the notion of logical possibility.

In order that a man should understand the word "mother" it is at least necessary that if a situation occurred in which mothers lacked some property which happens at present to be common and peculiar to them, the man *would* still apply the word to mothers and only to mothers.

Followers of Wittgenstein often talk as if they thought that the substitution of "is capable of applying the word w correctly" for "understands the word w", or for "attaches to the word w its common meaning", gets rid of any reference to logical modalities. But it doesn't.

(The substitution of "is capable of applying the word w correctly" for "applies the word w correctly" only takes care of the fact that a man may understand a word even if he has *in fact* never applied it. This however is an entirely different point from the one I have just tried to make.)

Moreover, the notion of understanding a word involves reference to more than logical modalities. For consider the following case. Suppose a man applies the word "shape" to things that have shape and only to those things. Suppose however that when asked to tell us the shape of a piece of land, he replies "About an acre". Clearly, we should say that by "shape" he meant size. Yet the properties "having shape" and "having size" are not only co-extensive but *necessarily* co-extensive. So in order that a man should understand the word "shape", he must be able, when asked to tell us the shape of a particular object, to mention a determinate falling under the determinable "shape" (to use W. E. Johnson's terminology),[1] and not a determinate falling under the determinable "size".

It follows that a satisfactory explanation of the notion of understanding a word, even in the sense of "understanding" that we are now considering, involves reference to the capacity to apply the word in question to things which *fall under a certain concept*. Hence, "is capable of applying a word correctly" does *not* get rid of reference to the notion of a concept, and *it in no way explains that notion*.[2]

The above example also shows that Carnap is wrong in claiming that the notion of understanding a word can be "explicated"[3] by the concept of intension,[4] where w and z are said to have the same intension if and only if they necessarily apply to the same things.[5]

Thus Carnap's semantics fails to perform one of the tasks which it has been constructed to perform.

2

I think that in the last Section I have shown, in a way which is quite independent of the difficulties connected with the Paradox of Analysis, that we must distinguish between the sense (that is, the meaning) of the phrase "the concept of a mother" and the sense of the phrase "the concept of a female parent". That is to say, we must distinguish between (*a*) the concept "the concept of a mother" and (*b*) the concept "the concept of a female parent" – for I have shown that it is logically possible to have concept (*a*) without having concept (*b*). I have thus shown that we must distinguish between *different* concepts of the *same* concept.

[1] W. E. Johnson, *Logic*, Pt. I (Cambridge, 1921), Ch. XI.

[2] In the present Chapter, as in other parts of this book, I sometimes use the word "notion" instead of the word "concept". I do so purely for stylistic reasons. "Notion", as I use the word, means concept, and is not intended to carry any "psychologizing" implications.

[3] "Explication" is Carnap's favourite word which enables him to evade the question whether he is analysing a "common idea" or giving a "rational reconstruction" of it. Cf. R. Carnap, *Logical Foundations of Probability* (Chicago, 1950), Ch. I.

[4] *Meaning and Necessity*, pp. 202–3.

[5] *Ibid.* p. 23.

I think therefore that I have succeeded in giving an independent justification of this distinction. If I may so express myself, I think I have shown that even if the paradoxes of opaque contexts did not exist, we should still have had to accept the distinction in question.

There remain however two difficult and important problems connected with this distinction, and we must now discuss them.

For reasons which will be clear shortly, I will now change my example. Consider the following two propositions:

  (α)   The concept of a man is identical with the concept of a rational animal;

  (β)   The proposition that Fido is a man is believed to be true by John.

(β) is a rather clumsy way of saying "John believes that Fido is a man". But it is a perfectly grammatical way of saying this, and the reason for choosing it will be clear presently.

Now my solution of the Paradox of Analysis is as follows. Just as we must distinguish between the sense of the phrase "the concept of a mother" and the sense of the phrase "the concept of a female parent", so we must similarly distinguish between the sense of the phrase "the concept of a man" and the sense of the phrase "the concept of a rational animal"; and those senses, as the two phrases occur in the sentence (α), are different. Hence, the Paradox of Analysis is solved.

But I have not so far given any account of how the phrase "the concept of a man", e.g., is used when it expresses a different concept of the concept of a man from that expressed by the phrase "the concept of a rational animal". I have shown that sometimes at any rate the two phrases *must* differ in meaning; but how *are* they used when they so differ?[1]

So far as I can see, one possible account would be to suppose that in (α) the *whole phrase* "the concept of a man" is syntactically simple, and that so is the phrase "the concept of a rational animal". I will concentrate on the former phrase; but the discussion will of course apply, *mutatis mutandis*, to the latter phrase also.

But in this case what is the connexion between the sense of the word "man" and the sense of the phrase "the concept of a man"? In other words, what is the connexion between the concept of a man and that particular concept of this concept? More specifically, how is it that in order to understand the phrase in question, as it occurs

[1] From now on I will always use the word "meaning" as synonymous with "sense".

in (α), one must understand the word "man"? *And that this is so is indisputable.*

Is it not a contradiction to suppose (1) that in (α) the phrase "the concept of a man" is syntactically simple, and (2) that yet in order to understand the phrase one must understand the word "man"?

In all other cases, so far as I can see, if an expression is syntactically simple, one need *not*, in order to know its sense, know the sense of any of its parts. In fact, this is what "syntactically simple" seems to *mean*. For example, in order to understand the word "catastrophe", one need not understand the word "cat"; in order to understand the expression "the word "dog"", one need not understand the word "dog", etc. etc.

And, it seems, it is precisely because this is so that one can't substitute, and wouldn't think of substituting, for "cat" in "catastrophe", a word which has the same meaning as "cat". Or in the expression "the word "dog"", a word which has the same meaning as "dog", e.g. the Polish word "pies", and so get, e.g., from "The word "dog" has three letters", "The word "pies" has three letters".

We should notice, however, that Quine is not right when he says:

The personal name buried within the first word of the statement:

(11)   'Cicero' has six letters,

e.g., is logically no more germane to the statement than is the verb 'let' which is buried within the last word.[1]

He is not right since the Polish translation of (11) *will* contain "the personal name buried within the first word of it".[2] (Also, it is surely odd to call the *expression* ""Cicero"" a "word".)

Hence, the relationship between ""Cicero"" and "Cicero" can't be quite the same as that between "letters" and "let". There is therefore *a* sense of "syntactically simple" in which the word "letter" *is* syntactically simple, but the expression ""Cicero"" is *not*.

I do not think however that this in any way affects my argument. For I am using "syntactically simple" in such a way that an expression, E, is syntactically simple with respect to a proper part of it, E', if and only if in order to understand E one need *not* understand E'.

---

[1] *Mathematical Logic*, p. 26. I retain Quine's numbering.
[2] The Polish translation is:
    "Cicero" ma sześć liter.

And I will say that an expression is syntactically simple if and only if it is syntactically simple with respect to each of its proper parts. This is not a perfectly precise explanation, but I think it makes the meaning of the term "syntactically simple", as I use it, clear enough. In this sense both "letters" and ""Cicero"", in ""Cicero" has six letters", are syntactically simple. Just as in order to understand "letters" one need not understand the verb "let" so also, in order to understand the sentence ""Cicero" has six letters", one need not understand the word "Cicero". (We may suppose, if we like, that this means "need not know to whom the name "Cicero" applies" – this point is here immaterial.)

And of course, as Quine rightly stresses, one cannot substitute "Tully" for "Cicero" in the sentence in question without turning the proposition expressed by it into a falsehood. In fact, I think that this follows from my explanation of "syntactically simple". That is to say, if an expression is syntactically simple in my sense, then I think it follows that the substitution for an expression which is a proper part of it of an expression which has the same reference will not be necessarily truth-preserving. And obviously one would not expect it to be so.

But let us return to (α). If what I have said above is right, then the phrase "the concept of a man", as the phrase occurs in (α), *cannot* be syntactically simple.[1] But then it is syntactically compound (or complex); and if so, how can its sense be different from the sense of the phrase "the concept of a rational animal"?

One possible answer to this question is that whilst the sense of the phrase "the concept of a man", as the phrase occurs in (α), is not syntactically simple, the word "man" in the phrase is used with its *oblique* sense.

---

[1] There are obvious points of similarity between Church's attempt (*op. cit.*) to give a Fregean solution of the Paradox of Analysis and my own attempt to do so. But Church does not discuss the problem whether such phrases as "the concept of a vixen" and "the concept of a female fox", when they occur in sentence (A) in the statement of the Paradox, are or are not syntactically simple. As a result he does not answer what seems to me to be the crucial question: *How* can the sense of the phrase "the concept of a vixen" be *different* from that of the phrase "the concept of a female fox", if the sense of the word "vixen" is the *same* as that of the expression "female fox"? In fact, if I understand him rightly, he seems to imply that the phrases in question *are* syntactically simple. Moreover, I cannot see that Church provides any independent philosophical justification for adopting a Fregean solution of the Paradox. For all that Church says, this may be just one of the several alternative ways of dealing with the Paradox.

This, if I understand him rightly, is Morton G. White's answer.[1]
He claims that in:

(1)   The concept of being a brother is identical with the
        concept of being a male sibling

the word "brother" and the expression "male sibling" are being
used obliquely. (He uses the word "attribute" instead of "concept",
but this is unimportant.)

It seems to me that White's claim is completely wrong. In (1)
the word "brother" *cannot* be used obliquely: for then its sense
would be the sense of the phrase "the concept of being a brother";
ex hypothesi, this phrase is not syntactically simple; so what is the
sense of the word "brother" *in it?* White would have to claim that
the word is here being used obliquely, that is, that its sense is the
sense of the phrase "the concept of being a brother". But this phrase
is not syntactically simple; so what is the sense of the word "brother"
here? White would have to claim that here the word has its oblique
sense; and so on *ad infinitum.* A clear example of an infinite regress!

One thing therefore is certain: Morton G. White has not solved
the Paradox of Analysis.

Let us now return to (α). Well, then, if the phrase "the concept
of a man" in (α) is not syntactically simple, and if the word "man"
is not being used in it obliquely, how *can* the Paradox of Analysis
be solved?

I think that we must now make a distinction which so far as I
know has never been made before, and which I believe is of crucial
importance in this connexion. We must distinguish between saying
that an expression is syntactically simple, in the sense explained,
and saying that an expression is syntactically *unitary.* In other words,
we must distinguish between the concept of being syntactically
simple and the concept of being syntactically unitary. But what
does "syntactically unitary" mean?

Before trying to explain it, I must go into the second serious
difficulty which is involved in our undertaking.

Consider:

(γ)   The concept of a man is instantiated;
(δ)   The concept of a rational animal is instantiated.

It seems to me that we *must* hold that the phrases "the concept of
a man" and "the concept of a rational animal" do *not* have different

[1] Morton G. White, "On the Church–Frege Solution of the Paradox of Analysis",
Philosophy and Phenomenological Research, vol. 8 (1948).

senses in (γ) and (δ). Why? Because the *reference* of (γ) *is* a function of the ordinary reference of the word "man", and hence the *sense* of (γ) must be a function of the ordinary *sense* of the word "man". The same applies, *mutatis mutandis*, to (δ). And since the ordinary senses of "man" and "rational animal" are the same, the senses of (γ) and (δ) must also be the same.

Now this in itself does not lead to any paradoxical conclusions. On the contrary, it seems quite right to suppose that (γ) is the same proposition as:

(γ')   There are men,

and that (δ) is the same proposition as:

(δ')   There are rational animals.

And clearly (γ') and (δ') are one and the same proposition.[1]

Would Frege have said that whilst the senses of (γ') and (δ') are the same, the senses of (γ) and (δ) are not the same, and hence that the sense of (γ') is different from the sense of (γ), and that of (δ') different from that of (δ)? Or would he have denied that the senses of (γ') and (δ') are the same? I do not think that Frege gives a clear answer to these questions, although I may be wrong.

I think however that I have shown that the senses of (γ) and (δ) *must* be the same.[2]

But to return to the main problem. Although the fact that the senses of (γ) and (δ) are the same does not in itself lead to any paradoxical conclusions, it does in my opinion constitute a serious difficulty for a Fregean theory of oblique sense. So far as I know, neither Frege nor Church ever mentions it.

The difficulty is this. We now have to say that it is only in *some* sentences that a phrase such as "the concept of a man" expresses a

---

[1] The point would be even clearer if one took instead of (γ') and (δ'), "There are vixens" and "There are female foxes": surely these are one and the same proposition.

[2] In any case we could take instead of (γ), (δ), (γ') and (δ') the following:

(γ°)   John instantiates the concept of a man;
(δ°)   John instantiates the concept of a rational animal;
($\gamma^{\circ'}$)   John is a man;
($\delta^{\circ'}$)   John is a rational animal.

So far as I can see, Frege would have claimed that ($\gamma^{\circ'}$) and ($\delta^{\circ'}$) are one and the same proposition. But if I understand him rightly, he also thought that (γ°) and ($\gamma^{\circ'}$) are one and the same proposition and that (δ°) and ($\delta^{\circ'}$) are one and the same proposition. It follows that he would have had to agree that (γ°) and (δ°) are one and the same proposition. And (γ°) and (δ°) would serve the purpose of my argument just as well as (γ) and (δ).

concept which is different from the concept expressed by the phrase "the concept of a rational animal"; i.e. we have to say that it is only in *some* sentences that the two phrases express *different* concepts of the concept of a man.

And the question now is: Can we distinguish the two kinds of sentence in a way which does not involve reference to the notion of opacity?

I *think* we can do so as follows. Let us say that in a sentence *S* an expression, *E*, is syntactically unitary with respect to a proper part of it, *E'*, if and only if it is logically impossible that a man who has the concept expressed by *E'* but has *not* got the concept expressed by *E* should be able to entertain the proposition expressed by *S*.

I do not think that this explanation is circular: it involves no reference to the notion of opacity. Of course, it does (if it is correct) secure the result that syntactically unitary expressions occur only in sentences which are opaque. But this is as it should be. The point is that the explanation itself does not involve reference to the notion of opacity.

Let us now apply this explanation to our examples.

Can a member of our imaginary community entertain the proposition:

> The concept of a mother is identical with the concept of a female parent?

Clearly, he cannot: for he does not have the concept "the concept of a female parent". But he *can*, in spite of not having that concept, entertain the proposition:

> The concept of a female parent is instantiated.

To entertain *this* proposition he must have the concept of a female parent, but need *not* have the concept "the concept of a female parent".

If this is right, then we must say that such phrases as "the concept of a man" sometimes express higher-order concepts but sometimes do not.

Now if an expression *E* is syntactically simple with respect to a sub-expression *E'*, then it is also syntactically unitary with respect to it; *but the converse of this does not hold.*

My theory, then, is that in (α) the phrase "the concept of a man" is syntactically unitary but not syntactically simple. In order to understand the phrase, as it occurs in (α), one must understand the word "man"; but one cannot entertain the proposition expressed by (α) unless one also possesses the concept "the concept of a man". And the same applies, *mutatis mutandis*, to the phrase "the concept of a rational animal" as it occurs in (α).

Let us now briefly consider (β). In order to understand the phrase "the proposition that Fido is a man", as the phrase occurs in (β), one must understand the sentence "Fido is a man"; but the phrase, as it occurs in (β), is syntactically unitary. To entertain the proposition expressed by (β), one must have the concept "the proposition that Fido is a man". But contrast (β) with:

The proposition that Fido is a man is true.

Here the phrase "the proposition that Fido is a man" is *not* syntactically unitary.

To sum up. I think that in (α) the sense of the phrase "the concept of a man" is different from the sense of the phrase "the concept of a rational animal". And this is so in spite of the fact that these phrases are *not* syntactically simple, and in spite of the fact that the word "man" and the expression "rational animal" are *not* being used in them obliquely.

The question: Are "man" and "rational animal" being used in the respective phrases in their *ordinary* senses? must be answered as follows. In order to understand the first phrase one must understand the word "man", and in order to understand the second phrase one must understand the expression "rational animal". But this does *not* imply, and it is *not* true, that the two phrases are not syntactically unitary. And it is only if these phrases were not syntactically unitary that the fact that the sense of the first phrase is different from the sense of the second phrase would violate Frege's principle. For Frege's principle must be understood to mean *not* that the sense of an expression which is not syntactically *simple* is a function of the senses of its constituents, but that the sense of an expression which is not syntactically *unitary* is such a function. In other words, in (α) "man" and "rational animal" are not used in their oblique senses, and are not used in their ordinary senses: each forms a part of a unitary expression.

We must also notice that the sense of (α) *is* a function of the sense of the unitary expression "the concept of a man" and of the sense of the unitary expression "the concept of a rational animal". Similarly, the sense of (β) *is* a function of the sense of the unitary expression "the proposition that Fido is a man".

I realize that Frege did not make a distinction between "simple" and "unitary". And I am not trying to find out what he "really" meant. What I am doing in this part of the work might be more appropriately described as an attempt to construct a theory of meaning which would incorporate what seem to me to be some of Frege's fundamental insights.

3

I will now briefly return to Wisdom's (1), (2) and (3) because we are at last in a position to bring out clearly the basic contradiction which is involved in his theory.

What he did was this. He thought that such phrases as "the concept of being a vixen" and "the concept of being a female fox" must be interpreted to mean "the concept expressed by the word "vixen"" and "the concept expressed by the expression "female fox"" respectively; and he thought that any sentence containing one or both of the latter phrases must be interpreted in accordance with Russell's theory of definite descriptions. This *compelled* him to hold that all his three sentences express the same proposition. But it also made it impossible for him to explain the difference between propositions like (3), which give analyses of concepts, and propositions like (1) and (2), which do *not* do so. He then, in order to get out of this difficulty, put forward the theory that although all his three sentences *say* the same thing, yet in order to understand sentence (3) a man must understand the word "vixen" and the expression "female fox", and in order to understand sentence (2) a man must understand the expression "female fox".

This, however, entails that in sentence (3) the phrases "the concept expressed by the word "vixen"" and "the concept expressed by the expression "female fox"" must *not* be interpreted as descriptive phrases in Russell's sense. (And similarly that in (2) the latter phrase must not be interpreted as a descriptive phrase in Russell's sense.)[1]

It follows that Wisdom's theory, which he stated on four separate occasions and which he thought to be of great importance, was that the phrases "the concept expressed by the word "vixen"" and "the concept expressed by the expression "female fox"", as these phrases

---

[1] By referring now to sentences (2) and (3) I mean, of course, (2) and (3) as rewritten in accordance with Wisdom's interpretation of the phrases "the concept of being a vixen" and "the concept of being a female fox".

occur in (3), both *are* and are *not* descriptive phrases in Russell's sense. Surely, as clear a contradiction as one can get!

The truth is very different. Proposition (1) contains the concept "the concept expressed by the word "vixen"" and the concept "the concept expressed by the expression "female fox"". It does *not* contain either the concept "the concept of being a vixen" or the concept "the concept of being a female fox". Proposition (2) contains the concept "the concept expressed by the word "vixen"" and the concept "the concept of being a female fox". It does *not* contain either the concept "the concept expressed by the expression "female fox"" or the concept "the concept of being a vixen". Proposition (3) contains the concept "the concept of being a vixen" and the concept "the concept of being a female fox". It does *not* contain either the concept "the concept expressed by the word "vixen"" or the concept "the concept expressed by the expression "female fox"".

If this sounds complicated, I can only plead that the truth of the matter *is* complicated.

Our investigation therefore shows that Wisdom has failed to solve the Paradox of Analysis. But I believe it shows more than this. I believe it also shows that Russellian semantics is incapable of solving it. For it is an essential feature of this part of Russell's semantics, that is, of his theory of definite descriptions, that even if a descriptive phrase has no denotation (i.e. no reference), a sentence in which the phrase occurs has meaning. But it is only if we interpret a phrase such as "the concept of being a vixen" as meaning "the concept expressed by the word "vixen"", and interpret the latter phrase so that in order to understand it a man need *not* understand the word "vixen", that we get this result. Otherwise the phrase "the concept of being a vixen" (e.g.) is simply *not* a descriptive phrase in Russell's sense.

4

We are now also in a position to bring out clearly the fundamental contradiction involved in C. I. Lewis's theory of meaning.

For consider:

(*a*)   There is no man who isn't rational;

(*b*)   There is no rational animal who isn't rational.

On Lewis's theory sentences (*a*) and (*b*) have different meanings although the word "man" and the expression "rational animal" have the same meaning. Hence, on Lewis's theory, the meaning of (*a*) is not a function of the meanings of its constituents (and similarly for (*b*)).

But if in (*a*) we substitute for the word "man" the expression "featherless biped", we get:

    (*c*)   There is no featherless biped who isn't rational.

This however still gives us a true proposition: more generally, the substitution for "man" in (*a*) of any expression which has the same reference as "man" is necessarily truth-preserving (and the same is true, *mutatis mutandis*, of (*b*)). Hence the *reference* of the sentence (*a*) *is* a function of the references of its constituent expressions, and the same is true of the reference of (*b*). But the supposition that the *reference* of a sentence *S is* a function of the references of its constituents and that yet the *meaning* of *S* is *not* a function of the meanings of its constituents is simply absurd.

Moreover, if we put the matter in Frege's terminology, then the contradiction in Lewis's theory will become quite obvious. For what Lewis's theory then comes to is this: that in (*a*) the word "man" has its *ordinary* reference but its *oblique* meaning; and similarly that in (*b*) the expression "rational animal" has its ordinary reference but its oblique meaning. And this is a contradiction. For meaning (sense) determines reference, and thus a word (or expression) which has oblique meaning must have oblique reference. *A fortiori*, a word (or expression) which has ordinary reference must have ordinary meaning.

5

So far as I can see, the only aspect of the matter which I have not explicitly discussed is this. Someone might say: Why not accept that (α) is the same proposition as:

    (α′)   The concept of a man is identical with the concept of a man?

That is, why not agree that true propositions which give analyses o concepts are trivial (in the sense that, e.g., (α) is identical with (α′)), but explain the usefulness of such propositions by saying that by using the *sentence* (α) the speaker implies, in some sense of "implies" which remains to be analysed, the corresponding synonymity proposition? In other words, it might be suggested that (α) does not *logically* imply anything about the word "man" or the expression "rational animal"; but that by asserting (α) the speaker implies, in some non-logical sense of "implies", that the word "man" is synonymous with the expression "rational animal". This, clearly, is *not* trivial, and this is the value of a philosophical analysis.

I should reply to this as follows. Quite apart from the obscurity of the alleged sense of "implies", why *should* one suppose that (α) is identical with (α')?

Obviously, the only argument for supposing so is as follows:
If

(1) (α) is true;
(2) in (α) "man" and "rational animal" are used with their ordinary senses;

and

(3) the sense of a compound expression is a function of the senses of its constituents;

then

(4) (α) is identical with (α').

We have seen that (2) is false; but what I now wish to point out is that if (2) is true, then it must also be true that

(2') in (α) "man" and "rational animal" are used with their ordinary references.[1]

At the same time, if (3) is true, then it must also be true that

(3') the reference of a compound expression is a function of the references of its constituents.

And this is so because it would be absurd to accept Frege's functionality-principle for sense and yet reject his functionality-principle for reference.

But then, since the reference of "rational animal" is the same as the reference of "featherless biped", it follows immediately that the reference of (α) is the same as the reference of:

(α'') The concept of a man is identical with the concept of a featherless biped.

But clearly it isn't: (α) is true, but (α'') is false. The concept of a man is not identical with the concept of a featherless biped, although the class of men is identical with the class of featherless bipeds. Otherwise sense would be identical with reference. And we have shown (see p. 85) that this is not so.

It follows immediately that the conclusion of the Paradox of Analysis cannot be accepted.

---

[1] That if (2) is true then (2') is true, is unquestionable.

8

Abstract entities and analyticity

Let us now return to what I called earlier[1] "justification" and symbolized by "⇒". Can we generalize this notion?

I think we can do as follows. Let us say:

P ⇒ Q if and only if P ⥽ Q, *and* only logical *or* semantical expressions occur in P and Q essentially.[2]

I am using "essential occurrence" in Quine's sense.[3] It is not necessary for my purpose to define this term precisely. Quine does so in his paper, to which the reader may be referred. Roughly, an expression occurs essentially in a sentence if replacement of the expression by another is capable of turning the proposition expressed by the sentence into a falsehood. (Cf. Quine, *Mathematical Logic*, Introduction.) Thus, to give Quine's own examples, the words "Socrates" and "man" occur essentially in the sentence "Socrates is a man", since "Bucephalus is a man" and "Socrates is a horse" express falsehoods. On the other hand, in the sentence "Socrates is mortal or Socrates is not mortal", the words "Socrates" and "mortal" do not occur essentially, but the logical particles "or" and "not" do occur essentially.

Under "logical particles" I include also the quantifiers, the identity sign, and modal particles, such as "logically possible" and "logically necessary".

Under "semantical expressions" I include "means" and "means the same as" – I shall not be concerned with other expressions which might be regarded as semantical and thus covered by the above definition.

[1] See Chapter 5.
[2] More accurately: P ⇒ Q if and only if P ⥽ Q, *and* only logical *or* semantical expressions occur essentially in sentences which express the propositions P and Q respectively.
[3] W. V. O. Quine, "Truth by Convention" in O. H. Lee (ed.), *Philosophical Essays for A. N. Whitehead* (New York, 1936). Reprinted in Quine's *The Ways of Paradox and Other Essays* (see esp. pp. 73ff.).

Although earlier on we read the symbol "⇒" as "justifies", let us now, for reasons which will be clear presently, read it as "structurally entails" and call the relation expressed by it "structural entailment".

I now wish to suggest that when it is said that necessary propositions are justified by, or based on, or owe their truth to, linguistic conventions, what is meant by this may be as follows. (A) That, e.g., the proposition ""Vixen" means the same as "female fox""(i.e. Wisdom's proposition (1)) ⇒ the proposition "The concept of being a vixen is identical with the concept of being a female fox" (i.e. Wisdom's proposition (3)). That is to say, that (1) ⊰ (3), and that in addition the expressions ""vixen"", ""female fox"", "vixen" and "female fox" do not occur in these sentences essentially. (B) That, e.g., the proposition ""Vixen" means female fox" (i.e. Wisdom's proposition (2)) ⇒ (3). (C) That, e.g., (1) ⇒ the proposition (4) "There is no vixen which is not a female fox". (D) That, e.g., (2) ⇒ (4). (E) That, e.g., (1) ⇒ the proposition (5) "It is logically necessary that there is no vixen which is not a female fox". (F) That, e.g., (2) ⇒ (5).

If this is what Wisdom and other conventionalists wish to maintain, then they are mistaken.

All of the following propositions are false:

(1) ⇒ (3);
(2) ⇒ (3);
(1) ⇒ (4);
(2) ⇒ (4);
(1) ⇒ (5);
(2) ⇒ (5).

I also believe that this notion of structural entailment will serve for certain philosophical purposes for which a relation narrower than strict implication is needed. And I therefore believe that the notion is of importance. I now think that it was a mistake to suppose that for those purposes it is necessary to distinguish between strict implication and entailment by denying that an impossible proposition entails any proposition and that a necessary proposition is entailed by any proposition.[1]

Structural entailment is of course an extension of what may be called "formal entailment",[2] where this is defined as follows:

[1] The problem of the relationship between strict implication and entailment is discussed at length in Chapters 9 and 10.   [2] Cf. Quine, "Truth by Convention".

P formally entails Q if and only if $P \dashv Q$, *and* only *logical* expressions occur in P and Q essentially.[1]

If we symbolize this by "$P \vdash Q$", we get:

If $P \vdash Q$ then $P \Rightarrow Q$, but not vice versa.

We can also define:

P materially entails Q if and only if $P \dashv Q$, *and* $\sim (P \vdash Q)$.

An example of a material entailment would be:

"My tie is red" materially entails "My tie is coloured".

An example of a structural entailment which is not also a formal entailment would be:

""Vixen" means the same as "female fox"" $\Rightarrow$ ""Female fox" means the same as "vixen"".

2

I shall now specify the propositions expressed by Wisdom's sentences (1), (2) and (3) in a way different from that in which I did so earlier on, and I shall also discuss some related problems.

First, let us reformulate (1), (2) and (3) as follows.

(1) The concept expressed by the word "vixen" is identical with the concept expressed by the expression "female fox";

(2) The concept expressed by the word "vixen" is identical with the concept of being a female fox;

(3) The concept of being a vixen is identical with the concept of being a female fox.

We can now give the following explanation of Wisdom's use of these sentences.

I. X is capable of entertaining the proposition expressed by sentence (1) (as Wisdom uses the sentence) if and only if

(A) X has the concept "the concept expressed by the word "vixen"";

(B) X has the concept "the concept expressed by the expression "female fox"";

(C) X has the concept of identity;

(D) X is capable of entertaining propositions of the form "x is identical with y"[2].

---

[1] More accurately: P formally entails Q, if and only if $P \dashv Q$, *and* only *logical* expressions occur essentially in sentences which express the propositions P and Q respectively.

[2] So far as I can see, (D) is not redundant in any of the sets I, II and III. But to discuss

II. X is capable of entertaining the proposition expressed by sentence (2) (as Wisdom uses the sentence) if and only if

    (A) X has the concept "the concept expressed by the word "vixen"";

    (B') X has the concept "the concept of being a female fox";

    (C) X has the concept of identity;

    (D) X is capable of entertaining propositions of the form "x is identical with y".

III. X is capable of entertaining the proposition expressed by sentence (3) (as Wisdom uses the sentence) if and only if

    (A') X has the concept "the concept of being a vixen";

    (B') X has the concept "the concept of being a female fox";

    (C) X has the concept of identity;

    (D) X is capable of entertaining propositions of the form "x is identical with y".

Let us now introduce the following notions.

    (α) P analytically entails Q if and only if $P \rightarrow_3 Q$, *and*, necessarily, anybody who is capable of entertaining P is capable of entertaining Q.

This is equivalent to:

P analytically entails Q if and only if $P \rightarrow_3 Q$, *and* Q contains no concepts which P does not contain.

    (β) P is analytically equivalent to Q if and only if P analytically entails Q, and Q analytically entails P.

This is equivalent to:

P is analytically equivalent to Q if and only if $P \equiv Q$, *and* P and Q contain the same concepts.

Let us symbolize "analytically entails" by "$\rightarrow$" and "is analytically equivalent" by "$\rightleftarrows$".

It is clear that "$P \rightleftarrows Q$" means that P and Q are one and the same proposition and that "$P \rightarrow Q$" means that the proposition Q is contained in the proposition P.

Let us now give a *new* (third) interpretation of Wisdom's notion of "making the same factual claims":

P and Q make the same factual claims if and only if $P \rightleftarrows Q$.

In other words, P makes no factual claims which Q doesn't make if and only if $Q \rightarrow P$; and Q makes no factual claims which P doesn't make if and only if $P \rightarrow Q$.

---

this would take us too far afield. Those who consider (D) redundant may leave it out: this would not affect my arguments.

In this interpretation Wisdom's position is as follows.

(A) (1) → (2);
(B) (2) → (1);
(C) (1) → (3);
(D) (3) → (1);
(E) (2) → (3);
(F) (3) → (2).

All of the above six assertions of Wisdom's are false.

(A) (1) ↛ (2).[1] *Proof.* (2) contains the concept "the concept of being a female fox" which (1) does not contain.

(B) (2) ↛ (1). *Proof.* (1) contains the concept "the concept expressed by the expression "female fox"" which (2) does not contain.

(C) (1) ↛ (3). *Proof.* (3) contains the concept "the concept of being a vixen" and the concept "the concept of being a female fox"; (1) does not contain either of these concepts.

(D) (3) ↛ (1). *Proof.* (1) contains the concept "the concept expressed by the word "vixen"" and the concept "the concept expressed by the expression "female fox""; (3) does not contain either of these concepts.

(E) (2) ↛ (3). *Proof.* (3) contains the concept "the concept of being a vixen" which (2) does not contain.

(F) (3) ↛ (2). *Proof.* (2) contains the concept "the concept expressed by the word "vixen"" which (3) does not contain.

I deliberately call these arguments "proofs" – they are absolutely conclusive.

It is clear that the notion of analytic entailment enables us to give yet another interpretation of conventionalism. In this interpretation conventionalism holds (*a*) that all logically necessary propositions are analytically entailed by the corresponding propositions of the type of Wisdom's (1); and (*b*) that all necessary propositions are analytically entailed by the corresponding propositions of the type of Wisdom's (2).

Since Wisdom's (3) is itself a logically necessary proposition, and yet is not entailed by (1) or by (2), it follows immediately that (*a*) and (*b*) are both false.

---

1 "↛" means "does not analytically entail".

Let us now consider

(4)   There is no vixen which isn't a female fox,

and ask the following two questions:

(I)   Does (1) analytically entail (4)?

(II)   Does (2) analytically entail (4)?

The answer to (I) is clearly in the negative: (4) contains the concept of being a vixen which (1) does not contain. The answer to (II) seems to me to be also in the negative. (4) contains the concept of negation and the concept of the existential quantifier whilst (2) does not contain either of these concepts.

We should notice, however, that even if this is wrong, and the answer to (II) is in the affirmative, this would still not entitle us to say that conventionalism involves *one* claim which is both true and non-trivial. For if (2) → (4), then also "Fido is a female fox" → (4). More generally, if (2) → (4), then *any* proposition which contains the concept of being a female fox analytically entails (4).

Perhaps this claim is not *as* trivial as the claim that (4) is entailed (i.e. strictly implied) by any proposition whatever; but it is still trivial.

In any case, I *don't* think that (2) analytically entails (4).

I am not offering the notion of analytic entailment as an acceptable reconstruction, let alone correct analysis, of the pre-formal, intuitive notion of logical entailment.

We have seen, however, that it is an important notion since mutual analytic entailment (i.e. analytic equivalence) enables us to elucidate the notion of propositional identity.

3

Let us now introduce two new operators, "$\Box$" to mean "it is analytically necessary that..." (or simply, "it is analytic that..."), and "$\Diamond$" to mean "it is analytically possible that...".

We then have:

(1) $\Box P$ if and only if $\sim \Diamond \sim P$;

(2) $\Diamond P$ if and only if $\sim \Box \sim P$.

Clearly, we also have:

(3) $\Box P \dashv \Box P$;[1]

(4) $\Diamond P \dashv \Diamond P$.

From (3) we get by contraposition:

(5) $\sim \Box P \dashv \sim \Box P$;

[1] "$\Box$" means "it is logically necessary that...".

and from (4) we get similarly:

(6)　　$\sim \Diamond P \dashv \sim \Diamond P.$

But the following are *not* in general valid:

(7)　　$\Box P \dashv \boxdot P;$
(8)　　$\Diamond P \dashv \Diamond P.$

Hence, the following are also *not* in general valid:

(9)　　$\sim \boxdot P \dashv \sim \Box P;$
(10)　　$\sim \Diamond P \dashv \sim \Diamond P.$

It is also clear that

(11)　　$P \to Q$ if and only if $\sim \Diamond (P \,\&\, \sim Q),$

which is equivalent to:

(12)　　$P \to Q$ if and only if $\Box (P \supset Q).$

Next we have:

(13)　　$P \rightleftarrows Q$ if and only if $\Box (P \equiv Q).$

Moreover, we have:

(14)　　$\Box [(x)(\phi x \supset \psi x)]$ if and only if $(x)(\phi x \to \psi x);$
(15)　　$\Box [(x)(\phi x \equiv \psi x)]$ if and only if $(x)(\phi x \rightleftarrows \psi x).$

It is clear that "$\Box [(x)(\phi x \equiv \psi x)]$" means that ϕ and ψ are one and the same property, and that "$\Box [(x)(\phi x \supset \psi x)]$" means that the property ψ is contained in the property ϕ.

Further, the following are also valid:

(16)　　$\Box P \dashv \Box \Box P;$
(17)　　$\Diamond P \dashv \Box \Diamond P.$

On the other hand, I think that the following are *not* in general valid:

(18)　　$\Box P \dashv \boxdot \Box P;$
(19)　　$\Diamond P \dashv \boxdot \Diamond P;$
(20)　　$\boxdot P \dashv \boxdot \boxdot P;$
(21)　　$\Diamond P \dashv \boxdot \Diamond P.$

If I am right in thinking that (20) and (21) are not in general valid, then perhaps some of those philosophers who rejected Lewis's axioms C10 and C11 had confused logical necessity with analytic necessity, and logical possibility with analytic possibility.

4

Finally, I think there is a connexion between my analytic entailment and W. T. Parry's "analytic implication".[1]

---

[1] W. T. Parry, "Ein Axiomensystem für eine neue Art von Implikation (analytische Implikation)", *Ergebnisse eines math. Kolloquiums*, no. 4 (for 1931–2).

As we shall see in Chapter 9, in Parry's system we do not have

P entails $(P \lor Q)$.

This disqualifies the system, in my opinion, from being an acceptable reconstruction of the intuitive notion of entailment. But it is exactly what we should expect if we identify entailment with my analytic entailment. For in a proposition expressed by a substitution instance of the above formula the consequent may well contain a concept not contained in the antecedent.

On the other hand, my analytic entailment is a narrower relation than Parry's: for in his system we have, e.g.,

P entails $\sim \sim P$,

which we do not have for my analytic entailment.

I do not therefore think that Parry's relation gives an acceptable analysis, or reconstruction, of "Q is contained in P", although it is, of course, an implication relation which holds on purely logical grounds.

We can now proceed as follows.

P synthetically entails Q if and only if

$P \dashv Q$, *and* $\sim (P \rightarrow Q)$.

(Let us symbolize this by "$P \multimap Q$".)

This will give us:

"This is red" $\multimap$ "This is coloured".

Also, if we write "$P \rightleftharpoons Q$" for mutual synthetic entailment (i.e. synthetic equivalence), we get:

"This has shape" $\rightleftharpoons$ "This has size".

Clearly, however, we also get, e.g.,

$P \multimap (P \lor Q)$,

and

$P \multimap \sim \sim P$,

and

$(P \& \sim P) \multimap Q$.

I think this is as it should be; but we could also introduce a different notion (let us call it material synthetic entailment and symbolize it by "$P \overset{m}{\multimap} Q$") as follows:

$P \overset{m}{\multimap} Q$ if and only if P materially entails Q, and $\sim (P \rightarrow Q)$.

That is, $P \overset{m}{\multimap} Q$ if and only if

(1) $P \dashv Q$,

(2) $\sim (P \vdash Q)$,

(3) $\sim (P \rightarrow Q)$.

I don't think, however, that this captures any notion of importance. For whilst material synthetic entailments will exclude, of course, those synthetic entailments which are also formal entailments, the following entailment, e.g., will *not* be excluded:

"Cambridge is larger than London" $\overset{m}{\prec}$ "There is nothing which is red and is not coloured".

I think that synthetic entailment as defined before ($\prec$) is the nearest we can get to the idea of a "synthetic necessary connexion".[1]

---

[1] The only other possibility which might perhaps be worth considering is to add the following two clauses to the definition of material synthetic entailment: (4) Q is purely contingent, and (5) $\sim P$ is purely contingent (in the sense of "purely contingent" which will be defined in Chapter 10).

9

Entailment: I

I shall now discuss the relationship between strict implication and our pre-formal ideas of logical entailment.

As I have already explained, Lewis defines "$P \dashv Q$" to mean "$\sim \Diamond (P \& \sim Q)$". And the *definiens* is of course equivalent to "$\sim \Diamond \sim (P \supset Q)$".

That is to say, P strictly implies Q if and only if the corresponding material implication is logically necessary.

It is obvious that, given Lewis's definition, a logically impossible proposition *strictly implies* any proposition whatever, and that a logically necessary proposition *is strictly implied by* any proposition whatever.[1]

These consequences of Lewis's definition have been called the "paradoxes of strict implication"; but they are paradoxical, in the sense of being counter-intuitive, *only if* strict implication is identified with our pre-formal, intuitive concept of entailment. For then we have to say that a logically impossible proposition *entails* any proposition whatever, and that a logically necessary proposition *is entailed by* any proposition whatever. And many philosophers and logicians have thought this counter-intuitive. Lewis was well aware of this. In fact at first he himself found these consequences counter-intuitive.[2] But later he changed his mind and claimed that they do not just depend on his definition, but can be proved by using principles which are true of the *intuitive* concept of entailment. In other words, he thought he could prove the allegedly paradoxical conclusions by relying only on assumptions about entailment that no one would question.

---

[1] In case this is not obvious to everybody, we can show it as follows: If P is itself impossible, the conjunction of P with any proposition whatever is also impossible; and if Q is itself necessary, then $\sim Q$ is impossible, and thus the conjunction of $\sim Q$ with any proposition whatever is also impossible.

[2] C. I. Lewis, "Implication and the Algebra of Logic", *Mind*, vol. 21 (1912).

I will now discuss his two "independent" proofs.

Proof A. This purports to show that an impossible proposition entails any proposition whatever.

	(1)	$P \, \& \sim P$;
(1) entails	(2)	P;
(1) entails	(3)	$\sim P$;
(2) entails	(4)	$P \lor Q$;
[(3) & (4)] entails	(5)	Q.[1]

Hence, assuming the transitivity of entailment, we get:

(6) $(P \, \& \sim P)$ entails Q.

In fact, Lewis did not explicitly state this last step and did not mention that an appeal to the transitivity of entailment is involved in the proof: he just assumed that entailment is transitive.

I have already pointed out that this proof, even if valid, proves less than Lewis takes it to prove: it proves at most that a contradiction of the propositional calculus entails any proposition whatever, *not* that *any* logically impossible proposition does so.

Lewis thought otherwise. Immediately after giving his proof, he goes on to say (pp. 250–1):

Thus any proposition one chooses may be deduced from the denial of a tautological or necessary truth: the theorem

$$\sim \Diamond \, p \, . \, \dashv \, . \, p \dashv q$$

states a fact about deducibility.

Lewis thus identifies logical necessity with tautologousness and logical impossibility with anti-tautologousness.[2] He seems to think, though wrongly, that in this he is following Wittgenstein's *Tractatus*.[3] In fact, in the Introduction to *Symbolic Logic* Lewis says that in the period since the publication of *Principia Mathematica* the nature of logical truth itself has become more definitely understood, largely through the discussions of Wittgenstein. And he continues (p. 24):

It [logical truth] is 'tautological' – such that any law of logic is equivalent to some statement which exhausts the possibilities; whatever is affirmed in logic is a truth to which no alternative is conceivable.

---

[1] Lewis and Langford, *Symbolic Logic*, p. 250.
[2] By "anti-tautologousness" I mean of course contradictoriness.
[3] Cf. our discussion in Chapter 5 from which it is clear that Wittgenstein's position was subtly but importantly different.

In view of the previous passage which I have quoted from Lewis, it is clear that he thinks that the two sentences separated by the semicolon express the same assertion: he is identifying "being a tautology", in Wittgenstein's sense, with "being a truth to which no alternative is conceivable"!

He also goes on to say that from the relation of mathematics to logic, it follows that mathematical truth is similarly tautological; and then adds a footnote (p. 24):

With the further detail of Wittgenstein's conceptions the present authors would not completely agree.

He thus clearly implies, though he does not expressly say so, that according to Wittgenstein (in the *Tractatus*) mathematics also consists of tautologies. And this view was also attributed to Wittgenstein by Miss Stebbing in 1933 in her lecture on "Logical Positivism and Analysis".[1] This is a complete misrepresentation: in the *Tractatus* Wittgenstein maintained that whilst logic consists of tautologies mathematics consists of *identities*.

But to return to Lewis's Proof *A*. As I have pointed out,[2] it is doubtful whether we can prove, without assuming that "entails" means the same as "strictly implies", that *any* impossible proposition entails a proposition of the form "$P \ \& \sim P$"; and if so, even if one accepted Proof *A*, this would not force one to accept Lewis's generalized definition of entailment. I stress this point because I think it has been overlooked by many writers on the subject.

Proof B.   This purports to show that a necessary proposition is entailed by any proposition whatever.

$$(1) \quad P;$$

(1) entails $(2) \quad (P \ \& \ Q) \vee (P \ \& \sim Q);$

(2) entails $(3) \quad P \ \& \ (Q \vee \sim Q);$

(3) entails $(4) \quad Q \vee \sim Q.$[3]

Once again, Lewis fails to state the final conclusion, namely

$$(5) \quad P \text{ entails } (Q \vee \sim Q),$$

and thus fails to bring out that he has assumed the transitivity of entailment.

And once again, he takes the proof to show that *any* necessary proposition is entailed by any proposition whatever. After giving his second proof he goes on to say that this is a paradigm in which

---

[1] *Proc. of the British Academy*, vol. 19 (1933), p. 62.   [2] See Chapter 5.

[3] Lewis and Langford, p. 251. In (2), (3) and (4) I have changed the order of the disjuncts, but this obviously doesn't matter.

P may be any proposition whatever, and Q may be so chosen as to give any desired tautology, $Q \lor \sim Q$; and then continues immediately (p. 251):

Thus tautologies in general are deducible from any premise we please: the theorem

$$\sim \Diamond \sim q \mathbin{.} \mathbin{\dashv} \mathbin{.} p \dashv q$$

states a fact about deducibility.

There can therefore be no doubt that he identifies necessity with tautologousness.

In fact, what Lewis's second proof proves is at most that any tautology of the propositional calculus is entailed by any premiss whatever.

It remains true, however, that many philosophers and logicians have thought even these weaker conclusions to be counter-intuitive. We must therefore discuss the two proofs in detail.

Let me first state more fully than Lewis does all the assumptions which are involved in those proofs.

Assumptions involved in Proof A

    (α)   (P & Q) entails P;   (α') (P & Q) entails Q;

    (β) P entails ($P \lor Q$);

    (γ)   If P entails Q, and P entails R, then P entails (Q & R);

    (δ) $[\sim P \mathbin{\&} (P \lor Q)]$ entails Q;

    (ϵ)   If P entails Q, and Q entails R, then P entails R.

Assumption (ϵ) is of course the assumption of the transitivity of entailment.

It is obvious that if all these assumptions are accepted, then Lewis's first proof is unchallengeable; hence, anyone who wishes to challenge it must challenge one or more of them.

Assumptions involved in Proof B

    (I) P entails $[(P \mathbin{\&} Q) \lor (P \mathbin{\&} \sim Q)]$;

    (II) $[(P \mathbin{\&} Q) \lor (P \mathbin{\&} \sim Q)]$ entails $[P \mathbin{\&} (Q \lor \sim Q)]$;

    (III) (P & Q) entails Q;

    (IV) Transitivity of entailment.

Once again, it is obvious that Lewis's second proof can only be challenged by challenging one or more of those assumptions.

Let me first discuss Proof B.[1] My reason for doing so is that this proof seems at first sight more "fishy" than Proof A.

---

[1] The material contained in the rest of the present Section of this Chapter, i.e. the comparison between Lewis's two proofs, was included in my lectures for the first time in the academic year 1963–64.

I believe that one's first reaction to Proof *B* would be to question assumption (I). What is it that makes one uncomfortable about (I)? Certainly

$$P \supset [(P \& Q) \vee (P \& \sim Q)]$$

is a tautology of the two-valued propositional calculus; but – one is inclined to say – principle (I) already assumes, in *some* sense, "$Q \vee \sim Q$", since it is only because "$Q \vee \sim Q$" is logically necessary that it is correct to suppose that *P* by itself strictly implies $[(P \& Q) \vee (P \& \sim Q)]$. Nobody would suppose, for instance, that *P* strictly implies $[(P \& Q) \vee (P \& R)]$. Hence – one is inclined to say – Lewis's second proof, which purports to show that "$Q \vee \sim Q$" is entailed by any premiss whatever, assumes at step (I) that "$Q \vee \sim Q$" is necessary. That is, Lewis can prove that *P* entails "$Q \vee \sim Q$" only because he has already assumed that "$Q \vee \sim Q$" is itself necessary. But this – one is inclined to say – is no good. In order to show that *P* entails *Q* we don't normally have to assume that *Q* is itself necessary. For example, in order to show that "$1 + 1 = 2$" entails "$(1 + 1) + 1 = (2 + 1)$" we don't have to assume that the latter proposition is itself necessary.

To put the point in a slightly different way. In Proof *B* Lewis professes to deduce the conclusion, $Q \vee \sim Q$, from the premiss *P*. But in fact he assumes that the conclusion is itself necessary at his very first move – namely when he deduces (2) from (1).

Suppose someone now said that we could reconstruct Lewis's proof like this. Insert before (I) the following principles:

(I′) $[P \& (Q \vee \sim Q)]$ entails $[(P \& Q) \vee (P \& \sim Q)]$;

(I″) If $(P \& Q)$ entails *R*, and *Q* is necessary, then *P* entails *R*;

(I‴) $(Q \vee \sim Q)$ is necessary;

and then continue Proof *B* as before.

But this reconstruction would be unacceptable to anyone who wishes to distinguish between entailment and strict implication: such a person would reject (I″) since obviously if suppression of necessary premisses were always permissible without destroying the relation of entailment, then we could immediately identify entailment with strict implication. (For example, since "$2 + 2 = 4$" is necessary, and the conjunction of "Caesar is dead" *and* "$2 + 2 = 4$" entails "$2 + 2 = 4$", it would follow immediately that "Caesar is dead" entails "$2 + 2 = 4$".)

If, on the other hand, we delete (I″) and (I‴), and merely

replace (I) by (I'), then we cannot get Lewis's final conclusion, namely that P entails "$Q \lor \sim Q$". Of course, we should still be entitled to assert that "$P \& (Q \lor \sim Q)$" entails "$Q \lor \sim Q$". But *this* is not in the least paradoxical.

Thus, so far as Lewis's Proof B is concerned, it would be possible to reject assumption (I) on the ground that universal suppressibility of necessary premisses should not be allowed. It is irrelevant, it could be claimed, that

$$P \supset [(P \& Q) \lor (P \& \sim Q)]$$

is a tautology of the two-valued propositional calculus. For if we assumed that to every two-valued tautology with material implication as the main connective there corresponds a true entailment proposition, then the identity of entailment with strict implication would follow immediately.

This, then, is a *possible* solution of Lewis's Paradox B. And it is *prima facie* plausible since it accords with our vague intuition that if P is to entail Q, then Q must follow from P: and if we are antecedently relying on Q's necessity, then P is in fact quite irrelevant. But as we shall see later, this *prima facie* plausible solution will not do in the end.

I will now examine Lewis's Proof A. First of all, I will say at once, although this anticipates certain matters which I have not yet discussed, that the solution, first advanced by Nelson,[1] of rejecting assumptions (α) and (α') – that is, Lewis's move from (1) to (2) and his move from (1) to (3) – will not do in the end since the paradoxes which I have myself discovered, and which I will discuss presently, do not involve those assumptions. Similarly Parry's solution,[2] which rejects assumption (β) – that is, Lewis's move from (2) to (4) – will not do for the same reason: my own paradoxes do not involve that assumption.

Moreover, if the trouble with Lewis's *second* proof is due to illegitimate suppression, then the trouble with his *first* proof must also somehow be due to illegitimate suppression since from the intuitive point of view it seems absurd to deal in one way with one of the proofs and in a radically different way with the other proof. But if so, then it is obvious that we must try, somehow or other, to

---

[1] E. J. Nelson, "Intensional Relations", *Mind*, vol. 39 (1930). Although I believe Nelson's solution to be mistaken, there is no doubt that his paper, at the time it was published, was of considerable importance.

[2] W. T. Parry, *op. cit.*

challenge assumption (δ). For it is only (δ), that is, Lewis's move from (3) and (4) to (5), that can plausibly be thought to involve some kind of illegitimate suppression: it is entirely clear that no illegitimate suppression, of any kind, is involved in any of the other assumptions.

Now if Lewis's Proof *B* suppresses "$Q \vee \sim Q$", i.e. the conclusion which he professes to deduce from his premiss, then his Proof *A* presumably suppresses the negation of his premiss, that is, Proof *A* presumably suppresses "$\sim (P \,\&\, \sim P)$". But does it really do so? Does Proof *A* suppress the *tautology* "$\sim (P \,\&\, \sim P)$" just as Proof *B* suppresses the *tautology* "$Q \vee \sim Q$"?

I do not think so, and I therefore believe that a careful comparison of the two proofs brings out something of considerable interest and importance.

We have seen that if in Proof *B* we add the suppressed tautology "$Q \vee \sim Q$" as a conjunct to the antecedent of assumption (I), that is, if we replace (I) by (I′), then no paradox will result. Hence, if the two proofs are entirely parallel, we ought to be able to avoid paradox in the case of Proof *A* by adding the allegedly suppressed tautology "$\sim (P \,\&\, \sim P)$" as a conjunct to the antecedent of assumption (δ), that is, by replacing (δ) by:

(δ')   [$\sim (P \,\&\, \sim P) \,\&\, \sim P \,\&\, (P \vee Q)$] entails *Q*.

But in fact the replacement of (δ) by (δ') still allows us to derive a paradox. For our new set of assumptions enables us to prove:

[$(P \,\&\, \sim P) \,\&\, \sim (P \,\&\, \sim P)$] entails *Q*.

The proof is as follows.

(1) [$(P \,\&\, \sim P) \,\&\, \sim (P \,\&\, \sim P)$] ent $(P \,\&\, \sim P)$[1] [(α), $P/(P \,\&\, \sim P)$, $Q/\sim (P \,\&\, \sim P)$].

(2) $(P \,\&\, \sim P)$ ent *P*   [(α)].

(3) *P* ent $(P \vee Q)$ [(β)].

(4) $(P \,\&\, \sim P)$ ent $(P \vee Q)$ [(2), (3), Transitivity].

(5) $(P \,\&\, \sim P)$ ent $\sim P$ [(α')].

(6) $(P \,\&\, \sim P)$ ent [$(P \vee Q) \,\&\, \sim P$]   [(4), (5), (γ)].

(7) [$(P \,\&\, \sim P) \,\&\, \sim (P \,\&\, \sim P)$] ent [$(P \vee Q) \,\&\, \sim P$]
      [(1), (6), Transitivity].

(8) [$(P \,\&\, \sim P) \,\&\, \sim (P \,\&\, \sim P)$] ent $\sim (P \,\&\, \sim P)$
      [(α'), $P/(P \,\&\, \sim P)$, $Q/\sim (P \,\&\, \sim P)$].

---

[1] "ent" will now be an abbreviation of "entails". I leave out those substitutions that are entirely obvious.

(9) $[(P \& \sim P) \& \sim (P \& \sim P)]$ ent $[(P \lor Q)$
$\& \sim P \& \sim (P \& \sim P)]$
$[(7), (8), (\gamma)].$

(10 $[(P \lor Q) \& \sim P \& \sim (P \& \sim P)]$ ent Q $[(\delta')].$

(11) $[(P \& \sim P) \& \sim (P \& \sim P)]$ ent Q
$[(9), (10), \text{Transitivity}].$

We must surely agree, however, that if the conclusion of Lewis's first proof is paradoxical, then (11) is also paradoxical.

What, then, is the explanation of this difference between the two proofs? Why is it the case that whilst the replacement of (I) by (I') in Proof *B* leads to no paradox, the replacement of (δ) by (δ') in Proof *A* still leads to paradox?

I believe that the answer is as follows.

Consider:

(I^t) $P \supset [(P \& Q) \lor (P \& \sim Q)]$

and

(I'^{t}) $[P \& (Q \lor \sim Q)] \supset [(P \& Q) \lor (P \& \sim Q)].$

Now both (I^t) and (I'^{t}) are of course tautologies of the two-valued propositional calculus. On the other hand in the three-valued calculus of Łukasiewicz,[1] the position is quite different: (I'^{t}) *is* a three-valued tautology (i.e. a tautology of the calculus) but (I^t) is *not* a three-valued tautology. That (I'^{t}) is a three-valued tautology can easily be verified in the usual way.[2] That (I^t) is not can be shown as follows.

Substitute 1 for P, and $\frac{1}{2}$ for Q:

$1 \supset [(1 \& \frac{1}{2}) \lor (1 \& \sim \frac{1}{2})]$
$1 \supset [\frac{1}{2} \lor (1 \& \frac{1}{2})]$
$1 \supset (\frac{1}{2} \lor \frac{1}{2})$
$1 \supset \frac{1}{2}$
$\frac{1}{2}.$

Similarly, of course,

$P \supset (Q \lor \sim Q)$

---

[1] See e.g. J. Łukasiewicz, *Elementy Logiki Matematycznej* (Warsaw, 1929), 2nd edn (Warsaw, 1958). English trans., *Elements of Mathematical Logic* (Oxford, 1963).

[2] Łukasiewicz's matrices are as follows.

$\supset$	0	$\frac{1}{2}$	1
0	1	1	1
$\frac{1}{2}$	$\frac{1}{2}$	1	1
1	0	$\frac{1}{2}$	1

$\sim$	
0	1
$\frac{1}{2}$	$\frac{1}{2}$
1	0

$\&$	0	$\frac{1}{2}$	1
0	0	0	0
$\frac{1}{2}$	0	$\frac{1}{2}$	$\frac{1}{2}$
1	0	$\frac{1}{2}$	1

$\lor$	0	$\frac{1}{2}$	1
0	0	$\frac{1}{2}$	1
$\frac{1}{2}$	$\frac{1}{2}$	$\frac{1}{2}$	1
1	1	1	1

1 is the designated value.

L M M

is *not* a three-valued tautology; but

$$[P \mathbin{\&} (Q \vee \mathord{\sim} Q)] \supset (Q \vee \mathord{\sim} Q)$$

is a three-valued tautology.

Consider now:

$$(\delta^t) \quad [\mathord{\sim} P \mathbin{\&} (P \vee Q)] \supset Q$$

and

$$(\delta'^t) \quad [\mathord{\sim} (P \mathbin{\&} \mathord{\sim} P) \mathbin{\&} \mathord{\sim} P \mathbin{\&} (P \vee Q)] \supset Q.$$

Here the position is entirely different: both are of course two-valued tautologies; but *neither* is a three-valued tautology, as can be seen if we substitute, in each case, $\frac{1}{2}$ for P and o for Q.

Similarly, of course, neither

$$(P \mathbin{\&} \mathord{\sim} P) \supset Q$$

nor

$$[(P \mathbin{\&} \mathord{\sim} P) \mathbin{\&} \mathord{\sim} (P \mathbin{\&} \mathord{\sim} P)] \supset Q$$

is a three-valued tautology.

What is the significance of all this? I believe it is as follows. Lewis's two proofs both involve suppression but in fundamentally different ways. Proof *B* suppresses the *premiss* "$Q \vee \mathord{\sim} Q$" at the move from (1) to (2). And if this premiss is *not* suppressed, no paradox arises. Proof *A*, on the other hand, suppresses no *premiss*. What it does "suppress" is the metalogical principle of bivalence (which we may also call the principle of the two-valuedness of logic), namely the principle that every proposition has one and only one of two truth-values, truth and falsity.

If the principle of bivalence is assumed, the addition of "$\mathord{\sim} (P \mathbin{\&} \mathord{\sim} P)$" to the antecedent of (δ) is redundant; if the principle is not assumed, the addition does not do the work which it was intended to do.

Given the principle of bivalence, every step that Lewis uses in Proof *A* is an intuitively acceptable entailment step. Consequently, Anderson and Belnap cannot get round that proof in the way they attempt – by claiming that (δ) is not a true entailment-proposition.[1] For *why* isn't it? The only reason one could give for this is that true entailment-propositions must not assume the principle of bivalence. And clearly such a claim has to be justified. (In no way does (δ) involve any "fallacy of relevance".)

The most one can say against (δ) is that we may wish so to define "P entails Q" that Q should follow from P with the help of the

---

[1] A. R. Anderson and N. D. Belnap, "Tautological Entailments", *Philosophical Studies*, vol. 13 (1962).

smallest possible number of extra premisses *or* principles.[1] But I will try to show presently that this, rather vague, idea cannot be carried out at all in certain cases which go beyond the propositional calculus.

It should also be noticed that

$$(P \,\&\, Q) \supset P,$$
$$(P \,\&\, Q) \supset Q,$$

and

$$P \supset (P \vee Q),$$

which correspond to the entailment-steps (α), (α') and (β) in Lewis's first proof, are all of them not only two-valued tautologies, but also three-valued tautologies. None of *those* steps involves suppression of any kind.

2

I shall now state certain paradoxes which I have myself discovered, and I shall try to explain in what ways they throw a different light on the problem of distinguishing between entailment and strict implication.

Paradox 1.[2] Consider:

   (A) The proposition expressed by the English sentence "There is no brother who is not male" is the proposition that there is no brother who is not male;

   (B) The proposition that there is no brother who is not male is necessary;

   (C) The proposition expressed by the English sentence "There is no brother who is not male" is necessary.

Derivation of the paradox

   (1) [(A) & (B)] entails (C).

   (2) (A) is contingent.

   (3) (C) is contingent.

---

[1] This will be discussed further in Chapter 10.

[2] This paradox I discovered early in 1949. Cf. the entry "Lewy on entailment" in G. E. Moore, *Commonplace Book 1919–1953* (London, 1962). Cf. also C. Lewy, "Entailment", *Aristotelian Soc. Suppl. Vol.* 32 (1958). My treatment of the problem here is completely different, however, from that in the above paper.

I should also mention that originally I formulated Paradox *1* by putting the quoted sentence in a foreign language. I did so in order to avoid the objection that (A) is not contingent. But in view of our discussion in Chapter 2 this device seems to me no longer necessary.

(4)   (B) is necessary.

(5)   If (1), (2), (3) and (4) then (A) entails (C).

Hence

(6)   (A) entails (C).

But

(7)   [(A) & (C)] entails (B).

(8)   If P entails Q, and P entails R, then P entails (Q & R).

(9)   If P entails Q, and Q entails R, then P entails R (transitivity of entailment).

(10) P entails P (reflexivity of entailment).

(11) If (6), (7), (8), (9) and (10) then (A) entails (B).

Hence

(12) (A) entails (B).

But (12) is paradoxical (in the sense of being counter-intuitive).

One is inclined to say: that the proposition expressed by "..." is the proposition that ... cannot entail that the proposition that ... is necessary. I shall argue in the end that we can do no better than to accept (12). But it is really no use to claim that there is nothing *prima facie* paradoxical about it. To do so would show, I think, what Wittgenstein used to call a "lack of nose for philosophy". And so far as I know, those who thought Lewis's results to be paradoxical, also thought (12) to be paradoxical. Certainly, Moore, Wisdom, von Wright, Geach and Anderson (and many others) all did.

It should be noticed that Paradox *1* does not use the principle:

(P & Q) entails P.

Similarly, it does not use the principle:

P entails (P ∨ Q).

It follows that the solution of Nelson and that of Parry are here inapplicable: one might put this by saying that Paradox *1* shows that the difficulty about entailment is not due to any difficulty about the strength of the propositional connectives "&" and "∨". Paradox *1* shows that the real source of the difficulty must lie elsewhere.

Let us then scrutinize the derivation of the paradox. First of all, let us look at step (5). For this obviously involves suppression, and it may be thought that the acceptance of (5) involves the acceptance of the principle which I have earlier labelled (I″), and which leads immediately to the identification of entailment with strict implication, namely the principle:

If (P & Q) entails R, and Q is necessary, then P entails R.

But this is not so. (If it were so, (2) and (3) would be redundant.) Step (5) involves a more restricted principle, namely:

If (P & Q) entails R, and Q is necessary, and P is contingent, and R is contingent, then P entails R.

This more restricted principle seems intuitively acceptable. In fact, it may be recalled that Strawson *defines* "P entails Q" to mean:

(a) $P \dashv Q$,

(b) P is contingent,

(c) Q is contingent;

and from this the restricted principle follows immediately. Of course Strawson's definition has the obviously unacceptable consequence that entailment holds between contingent propositions only. But the restricted principle does not have this consequence, and it does not commit us to the acceptance of Strawson's definition. The principle merely states that the conjunction of (a), (b) and (c) forms a *sufficient* condition for the truth of "P entails Q", *not* that it forms a necessary condition. And this does seem intuitively acceptable.[1]

Let us look at the other steps. It seems entirely clear that steps (1), (2), (3), (7) and (11) must all be accepted; and I have already argued in favour of Lewis's C10 from which it follows immediately that step (4) must also be accepted. Next, of the three formal principles which are involved – (8), (9) and (10) – I think it would be entirely unprofitable to question either (8) or (10). Take first (8): this only states that it is a *sufficient* condition for "P entails (Q & R)" that P should entail Q and that P should entail R.[2] To deny this seems to me entirely counter-intuitive.

So far as (10) goes, the position is, if anything, even clearer: from the intuitive point of view entailment is reflexive.

This appears to have been denied by Moore. In his paper "Russell's 'Theory of Descriptions'"[3] Moore asserts that if we were to say "The proposition "The King of France is bald" both entails and is entailed by the proposition "Le roi de France est

[1] In fact, the derivation of Paradox *1* could be reformulated in such a way as to rely on a still weaker principle which would impose a further restriction on R, namely that R must be "purely contingent" in the sense which I will try to explain in Chapter 10. With this further restriction the principle seems even more acceptable. But for the present I will leave this aspect of the matter aside.

[2] I will call (8) the principle of adjunction.

[3] In P. A. Schilpp (ed.), *The Philosophy of Bertrand Russell* (Evanston & Chicago, 1944). Reprinted in G. E. Moore, *Philosophical Papers* (London, 1959).

chauve"", we should be definitely misusing the expression "both entails and is entailed by".[1] It follows that if we were to say "The proposition "The King of France is bald" entails the proposition "The King of France is bald"" we should be "definitely misusing" the word "entails". And if so, it would seem to follow that entailment is not reflexive.

I believe Moore was mistaken. I think he must have temporarily fallen into the trap, into which other philosophers have also fallen, of failing to distinguish between asserting of a certain sentence that it would not normally be used in everyday life, and asserting of it that it is meaningless in the sense of being ill-formed. The sentence "The proposition "The King of France is bald" entails the proposition "The King of France is bald"" is patently well-formed; if so, it expresses a proposition which is either true or false (I assume, of course, the principle of bivalence); and it would be absurd to suppose that it expresses a false proposition.[2]

If steps (1), (2), (3), (4), (7), (8), (10) and (11) must all be accepted, then we are left with only two possibilities: (*a*) we can deny that suppression is legitimate even in this special case, i.e. we can reject, after all, step (5); (*b*) we can reject step (9), i.e. we can deny that entailment is unrestrictedly transitive.

For many years my own position was that we must distinguish between *two* senses of "entails", in one of which (9) is true but (5) is false, and in the other of which (5) is true but (9) is false.[3]

It is clear that this second idea of mine, that in one sense of "entails" entailment is not unrestrictedly transitive, inspired T. J. Smiley's interesting attempt to formalize this concept in an article to which I shall refer again presently.[4] I believe that von Wright's definition of entailment[5] which I shall discuss in detail later on in this Chapter was also influenced by his knowledge of the Paradoxes *1* and *2*[6] which I communicated to him in a number of discussions in the middle 1950s – discussions to which he refers in the Preface to his book. But von Wright did *not* accept my first idea, namely that in *another* sense of "entails" entailment *is* unrestrictedly transi-

---

[1] *Philosophical Papers*, p. 180.
[2] Moore appears to have realized his mistake a few years later. Cf. the entry (written *c.* 1949) on "Laws of contradiction and excluded middle" in his *Commonplace Book*.
[3] See my 1958 paper mentioned earlier on.
[4] T. J. Smiley, "Entailment and Deducibility", *Proc. Aristotelian Soc.*, vol. 59 (1959).
[5] In the paper "The Concept of Entailment" first published in G. H. von Wright, *Logical Studies* (London, 1957).   [6] Paradox 2 will be given presently.

tive. And it is odd that he does not mention in his paper that if his definition is to avoid the paradoxes – Lewis's as well as mine – the relation defined by it must lack unrestricted transitivity.

P. T. Geach in his 1958 paper adopted a modified version of von Wright's definition,[1] and used it explicitly to solve my Paradoxes *1* and *2*. He thus accepted my second idea, but not my first idea.

On the other hand, my *first* idea recurs in Anderson and Belnap's attempt to construct a system of entailment, although the point of origin of their system was obviously W. Ackermann's paper. At any rate, Anderson and Belnap retain unrestricted transitivity but disallow suppression, and in this way their system has an obvious similarity to one of the suggestions in my 1958 paper.[2]

I should perhaps also add that I *never* thought that my second sense was the *primary* sense of "entails": I have *always* thought that it was only a secondary sense. And it was for this reason that I called the second sense "necessitation", and reserved the word "entailment" for the first sense. I thought that it is the first sense that we have in mind when we say that one proposition *taken alone* (or taken by itself) entails another; but I thought that there is also a *wider* sense of "entails" in which we should be willing to say in a certain kind of case that one proposition entails another, even if it does not do so taken alone but only in conjunction with another proposition which is itself necessary; and I thought that in this wider, secondary, sense entailment is not unrestrictedly transitive.

---

[1] P. T. Geach, "Entailment", *Aristotelian Soc. Suppl. Vol.* 32 (1958). Reprinted in P. T. Geach, *Logic Matters* (Oxford, 1972). Von Wright's definition (or truth-condition) is as follows: *P* entails *Q*, if and only if, by means of logic, it is possible to come to know the truth of $P \supset Q$ without coming to know the falsehood of *P* or the truth of *Q* (*op. cit.* p. 181). Geach's is as follows: There is an *a priori* way of getting to know that $P \supset Q$ which is not a way of getting to know either that $\sim P$ or that *Q* (*op. cit.* p. 165).

Apart from two differences which are obvious, and which Geach expressly mentions, the definitions are identical.

[2] Anderson and Belnap, *op. cit.* (Cf. also Anderson and Belnap, "The Pure Calculus of Entailment", *Journal of Symbolic Logic*, vol. 27 (1962).) But in the former paper they *patently* misrepresent me when they say, without mentioning at all my *first* idea, that I have recommended giving up the transitivity of entailment. (And they also attribute this "recommendation" to Smiley!) There is now substantial literature on the Anderson–Belnap system. Ackermann's paper referred to above is "Begründung einer strenger Implikation", *Journal of Symbolic Logic*, vol. 21 (1956). I should also add that Anderson and Belnap would presumably wish to avoid my Paradox *1* by rejecting step (5), that is, by alleging that the trouble is due to illegitimate suppression – just as I myself maintained in my 1958 paper for what I then thought was *one* sense of "entails".

I must now return to step (4) in the derivation of Paradox *1*. I have already pointed out that this step depends on the assumption that Lewis's C10 is intuitively acceptable. I believe it would be fair to say that in the 1950s this was more controversial than it is now; and early in 1954 I constructed a paradox which does not involve this dependence.[1]

Paradox 2. Take:

(A′)   Caesar is dead $\equiv$ Russell is a brother;
(B′)   Russell is a brother $\equiv$ Russell is a male sibling;
(C′)   Caesar is dead $\equiv$ Russell is a male sibling.

Here it is quite clear that (B′) is necessary and the necessity of it does not depend on the acceptance of C10.

The paradoxical conclusion, namely that (A′) entails (B′), can be derived in precisely the same way as (12) in Paradox *1*. (Substitute, in the derivation of Paradox *1*, (A′) for (A), (B′) for (B) and (C′) for (C).)

Paradox *2* is however awkward for a different reason. I should claim that the proposition "Russell is a brother" is identical with the proposition "Russell is a male sibling"; and I should also claim that it follows from this that the proposition (A′) is identical with the proposition (C′). But if so, then (*a*) we can get step (6) at once (i.e. there is no need for the first five steps),[2] and (*b*) the final conclusion, namely that (A′) entails (B′), comes merely to this: that "Caesar is dead $\equiv$ Russell is a brother" entails "Russell is a brother $\equiv$ Russell is a brother"; and I now think that this, although still counter-intuitive, is less counter-intuitive than that (A) entails (B).[3]

It is, however, quite easy to get round this by the following modification of Paradox *2*.

Paradox 3. Consider:

(A″)   Caesar is dead $\equiv$ this has shape;
(B″)   This has shape $\equiv$ this has size;
(C″)   Caesar is dead $\equiv$ this has size.

---

[1] Cf. C. Lewy, *op. cit.* I first gave it in lectures in the academic year 1953–54.

[2] By referring to steps (1)–(6) I mean, of course, the steps as revised by making the substitutions mentioned in the previous paragraph.

[3] Cf. P. Downing, "Entailment", *Proc. Aristotelian Soc.*, vol. 66 (1965–6). Downing, however, thinks that the conclusion of Paradox *2* is not counter-intuitive at all, and with this I disagree. Moreover, according to his definition of entailment, as he explicitly points out, the conjunction of (A) and (C) does *not* entail (B). But this consequence, I should say, is a conclusive reason against accepting his definition.

Then substitute, in the derivation of Paradox *1*, (A″) for (A), (B″) for (B) and (C″) for (C).

Here it is clear that the proposition "This has shape" is not identical with the proposition "This has size", and hence that the proposition (A″) is not identical with the proposition (C″). (Strictly speaking, the sentences "This has shape" and "This has size" do not by themselves express any propositions; but let us assume that the man uttering the sentences is pointing at a particular object.) And to suppose that "Caesar is dead ≡ this has shape" entails "This has shape ≡ this has size", seems to me just as counter-intuitive as to suppose that (A) entails (B).[1]

We are still left with the possibility of rejecting the unrestricted transitivity of entailment. But in order to show something which I believe to be very important in this connexion, and also for other reasons which will become clear later, I wish to state first another paradox which I discovered, or invented, in the summer of 1969.[2]

Paradox 4. Consider:

    (1)   There are exactly ten brothers;

    (2)   There are exactly as many brothers as brothers.

Now the following principles seem clearly acceptable:

    (A)   *P* entails (*P* & *P*);

    (B)   If *P* entails *Q*, and *Q* entails *R*, then *P* entails *R*;

    (C)   "There are exactly *n* ϕs and there are exactly *n* ψs" entails "There are exactly as many ϕs as ψs".

Given these principles, we get:

    (I)   (1) entails [(1) & (1)] [by (A)].

    (II)   [(1) & (1)] entails (2) [by (C)].

    (III)   (1) entails (2) [by (B)].

But (III) seems counter-intuitive.

Now it may be said that (III) is less counter-intuitive than the conclusions of Lewis's two proofs, or the conclusions of my paradoxes *1* and *3*.[3] I think this is true; but it shows that counter-

---

[1] Downing, in the paper already referred to, suggests a similar modification of Paradox *2*; but it is clear that he would say that (A″) does entail (B″). (Although, according to him, (A) does not entail (B).)

[2] It was first included in my seminar on philosophical problems of logic at Yale University in the autumn semester of 1969–70, and then in my Cambridge lectures in 1970–71.

[3] I will now leave aside Paradox *2* because of its connexion with the notion of propositional identity.

intuitiveness is a matter of degree, and that the distinction between what is counter-intuitive and what is not, is thus less sharp than entailment-theorists have supposed. In any case, I believe that *4* is at least a *mild* paradox.[1]

But clearly, Paradox *4* still assumes that entailment is unrestrictedly transitive; and it will not therefore appeal to philosophers like von Wright and Geach who deny this.

Let us therefore now discuss the view that entailment is *not* unrestrictedly transitive.[2]

What *is* the basic idea underlying this approach? I have no doubt at all that it is this. We want our knowledge that P entails Q not to rely on any antecedent knowledge of the modal values of the propositions involved. The relation between P and Q that we think we have in mind when we say that P entails Q must not be based on the modal value of P or that of Q. This vague idea is clearly

---

[1] In my 1964 paper "Entailment and Propositional Identity", *Proc. Aristotelian Soc.*, vol. 64 (1963–4), I gave six paradoxes which I labelled I–VI. I now think that that paper was extremely confused. In particular, I now think that if entailment is a relation between *propositions*, then the respective conclusions of Paradoxes I–IV must be accepted. The only other comment I have to make on those four paradoxes is as follows. Several philosophers who had read the paper thought that the conclusions in question *are* paradoxical; and this seems to me to go some way to show that over and above the difficulties which I am discussing in this Chapter, we have a tendency to oscillate between holding that the terms of the entailment relation are propositions and holding that they are "entities" of some sort which involve reference to *expressions*. I should now say that it is this fact that my Paradoxes I–IV of the 1964 paper bring out, if they bring out anything at all. But as I have just said, *if* entailment is a relation between propositions, then Paradoxes I–IV must be accepted. It should perhaps also be mentioned that those paradoxes do not assume the transitivity of entailment.

With respect to Paradoxes V and VI the position seems to me to be different. My discussion of them in the paper referred to was entirely wrong; but their respective conclusions still seem to me mildly paradoxical. I now think, however, that my new Paradox *4* brings out in a much better and simpler way, and without any reference to the notion of propositional identity, the main point underlying those two paradoxes. Moreover, we can now also construct another paradox, similar to Paradox *4*, but related to Paradox *2*. It is this. Take (α) "Caesar is dead $\equiv$ Russell is a brother", and (β) "Russell is a brother $\equiv$ Russell is a brother". Assume premisses (A) and (B), as in Paradox *4*; but instead of (C), assume

(C′) $[(P \equiv Q) \& (P \equiv R)]$ entails $(Q \equiv R)$.

Then, by a proof entirely analogous to that of (III) in Paradox *4*, we get that (α) entails (β). But I will not discuss this paradox further because it seems to add nothing of substance to Paradox *4*. Also, some entailment-theorists reject (C′).

[2] The reason why I wished to state Paradox *4* before discussing this matter will become apparent later.

present in such writings as my 1950 paper,[1] Moore's *Commonplace Book* (p. 271),[2] and von Wright's paper.[3]

It is intuitively very compelling. But what the paradoxes show is that entailment which tries to capture this idea, if it is really to work, will lack unrestricted transitivity.

A definition which attempts to formalize the basic idea that I am talking about is given in Smiley's paper:

$A_1, \ldots, A_n \vdash B$ if and only if $A_1 \& .. \& A_n \supset B$ is a substitution instance of a tautology $A'_1 \& .. \& A'_n \supset B'$, such that neither $\vdash B'$ nor $\vdash \sim (A'_1 \& .. \& A'_n).$[4]

Let us put this less exactly, but in a way which is a little clearer and will do for our purpose:

P entails Q if and only if $P \supset Q$ is a substitution instance of $P' \supset Q'$ such that (1) $P' \supset Q'$ is tautologous, (2) Q' is *not* tautologous, and (3) $\sim P'$ is *not* tautologous.

Smiley is only concerned with the propositional calculus; but I think that by substituting "logically necessary" for "tautologous", we can generalize his definition as follows:

P entails Q if and only if $P \supset Q$ is a substitution instance of $P' \supset Q'$ such that (1) $P' \supset Q'$ is logically necessary, (2) Q' is *not* logically necessary, (3) $\sim P'$ is *not* logically necessary.

This relation, however, is not unrestrictedly transitive – as of course Smiley points out.

For recall Lewis's Proof *A*:

	(1)	$P \& \sim P$;
(1) entails	(2)	P;
(1) entails	(3)	$\sim P$;
(2) entails	(4)	$P \vee Q$;
[(3) & (4)] entails	(5)	Q.

Hence, by transitivity,

(6) $(P \& \sim P)$ entails Q.

Each of the steps from (1) to (5) is a valid entailment-step on Smiley's definition. Yet the final conclusion (6) does *not* satisfy the

[1] "Entailment and Necessary Propositions", cited earlier.
[2] Moore does not apply the idea *directly* to entailment, but the application is fairly obvious.
[3] "The Concept of Entailment", cited earlier.
[4] "Entailment and Deducibility", p. 240.

"$\vdash$" symbolizes the entailment relation; in the above Smiley also uses "$\vdash$", but with nothing standing in front of it, to mean that what follows it is a tautology.

definition: $(P \& \sim P) \supset Q$ is of course a tautology, but it is not a substitution instance of a tautology of the required kind. It follows immediately that transitivity fails for this relation.

If we can generalize Smiley's definition in the way I have suggested, then my Paradoxes *1, 3* and *4* can also be solved by rejecting unrestricted transitivity of entailment.

In my opinion, von Wright's definition of entailment fails to solve even Lewis's paradoxes;[1] but it is clear that it can solve them *only if* the relation defined by it is not unrestrictedly transitive.

I should perhaps also mention that Geach in his 1970 paper on entailment[2] adopts what is essentially Smiley's definition, although he expresses it differently. And he says, quite rightly, that the relation thus defined is obviously non-transitive.

It is therefore clear that Smiley's definition avoids Lewis's paradoxes. But is it a correct analysis of the intuitive, pre-formal concept of logical entailment?

I do not think so.[3] My reasons are as follows.

1. I believe that it is *more* counter-intuitive to reject unrestricted transitivity of entailment than to identify entailment with strict implication. For the former course dissociates the notion of "*P* entails *Q*" from that of "There is a valid deductive proof of *Q* from *P*". Obviously, if there is a valid deductive proof of *Q* from *P*, and a valid deductive proof of *R* from *Q*, then there is a valid deductive proof of *R* from *P*. *This* is undeniable: proof *is* transitive. But intuitively "There is a valid deductive proof of *Q* from *P*" seems a sufficient condition for "*P* entails *Q*".[4] And I think this is a *very strong* intuition – one which we should be extremely unwilling to give up. In fact, if entailment is *not* unrestrictedly transitive, then *either* "*P* logically entails *Q*" is *not* the converse of "*Q* logically follows from *P*", *or* the latter has two different senses: for in at least *one* sense of "*Q* logically follows from *P*", this is obviously synonymous with "There is a valid logical (i.e. deductive) proof of *Q* from *P*". The suggestion that on the intuitive level "*P* logically

---

[1] For a detailed discussion of von Wright's definition see the last Section of this Chapter.

[2] P. T. Geach, "Entailment", *The Philosophical Review*, vol. 79 (1970). Reprinted in P. T. Geach, *Logic Matters* (Oxford, 1972).

[3] Neither did Smiley.

[4] I made this point in 1958 at Southampton in the discussion which followed the symposium on entailment; in discussions with von Wright a little later; and in my lectures in 1963–64 and some subsequent years.

entails Q" is *not* the converse of "Q logically follows from P" is highly implausible; and the second suggestion leads immediately to a theory which is weaker than that held by von Wright and by Geach, namely the theory that there are *two* concepts of entailment.[1]

We must also not forget that since proof *is* transitive (even if entailment is not), Lewis *has* given a valid deductive proof of Q from $(P \& \sim P)$. And von Wright and Geach are still left with this proof.

2. Although, on Smiley's definition, P does not entail $(Q \lor \sim Q)$, P does entail the *conjunction* $[P \& (Q \lor \sim Q)]$. More generally, on Smiley's definition, if P entails R, then P entails $[R \& (Q \lor \sim Q)]$. This is also counter-intuitive.[2]

3. Paradox *4* still assumes the unrestricted transitivity of entailment. But I think that it shows something which is of considerable importance in this connexion. It is certainly plausible to suppose that Smiley's definition captures, on the level of the propositional calculus, the intuitions which underlie von Wright's approach, and which, as I have already pointed out, were also expressed, although in a much vaguer form, in my 1950 paper and in Moore's *Commonplace Book*. In fact, Anderson and Belnap say explicitly that Smiley's criterion "gives rise to a definition of entailment" which is effectively decidable, and seems also "to capture the intent of von Wright and Geach".[3] And Geach, in his 1970 paper already cited, clearly shares this opinion. But in fact the matter is far more complex. I have already pointed out that Smiley's definition avoids Lewis's paradoxes; and I will show later that von Wright's definition does *not* avoid them. It follows immediately that the two definitions are different.[4] But then to say that Smiley's definition "captures von Wright's intent" is rather vague: perhaps even if Smiley's definition does avoid Lewis's paradoxes and von Wright's definition does not, the former "captures the intent" of the latter. But I will now show something which is highly relevant in this connexion. I will show

[1] Cf. my 1958 paper on "Entailment" and the entry "Lewy on entailment" in Moore's *Commonplace Book*.

[2] That this would be the consequence of any theory of entailment which attempted to capture the idea that entailment must not be "based" on the modal values of the two constituent propositions, I saw already in 1958 – before Smiley's paper was published. Cf. my 1958 paper.

[3] *Op. cit.* p. 10. I shall not in this connexion make any distinction between "definition", "truth-condition" and "criterion".

[4] I will later also give a case going beyond the propositional calculus in which the breakdown of von Wright's definition is absolutely patent.

that von Wright's definition does *not* avoid Paradox *4* whilst Smiley's definition (in its generalized form – otherwise it is inapplicable to the Paradox) does avoid it. And I shall then consider the *further* question whether this is merely another instance of the *general* failure of von Wright's definition to do the work which it was designed to do, or whether there is something more behind it.

That Smiley's definition (in its generalized form) does not allow us to derive (III) in Paradox *4* can be shown as follows. In order to derive (III) an appeal to the transitivity of entailment is essential (assumption (B) in the derivation of the paradox); and Smiley's restriction rules out transitivity in this very case. For "There are exactly ten brothers ⊃ there are exactly as many brothers as brothers" is not a substitution instance of any material implication which satisfies *both* condition (1) *and* condition (2) of the generalized definition. It *is* a substitution instance of:

There are exactly n ϕs ⊃ there are exactly as many ϕs as ψs,

but this does not satisfy condition (1); and it is also a substitution instance of:

There are exactly n ϕs ⊃ there are exactly as many ϕs as ϕs,

but this does not satisfy condition (2).

On the other hand, that von Wright's definition (even in Geach's modified version) does allow us to derive (III) in Paradox *4* can be shown as follows. Proposition (2) in the Paradox is of course logically necessary; but it is *not* the case (to use here Geach's language rather than von Wright's) that there is no *a priori* way of getting to know that (1) materially implies (2) which is not also a way of getting to know either that it is false that there are exactly ten brothers or that it is true that there are as many brothers as brothers. There *is* such a way: it is given by my proof.

Let us now ask the following question: Is this difference between the two definitions merely another instance of von Wright's *general* failure to define a relation which is narrower than strict implication? I do not really think so; but the question is subtle, and since we are now working on a rather deep intuitive level, it is difficult to give an answer which will carry full conviction. But I will try to do so. As I have already stressed – and I feel certain that he would not dispute it – the basic idea of von Wright's approach, which his definition (or truth-condition) was designed to capture, is the idea that we should so define "*P* entails *Q*" that the truth of this does not "depend" on the modal value of *P* or the modal value of *Q*.

Now it seems to me that on the intuitive level there is a funda-mental difference between (*a*) Lewis's paradoxes and my own Paradoxes *1* and *3* on the one hand, and (*b*) my Paradox *4* on the other hand. Let me try to explain this. First, let me compare Paradoxes *1* and *3* with those of Lewis's. In one respect *1* and *3* differ from *both* Lewis's paradoxes in that Lewis's are on the level of the propositional calculus, whilst *1* and *3* go beyond it. But in another respect, *1* and *3* resemble Lewis's *second* paradox rather than his first: namely, both *1* and *3* suppress a necessary *premiss* rather than a metalogical principle.[1] Now in this respect, too, Paradox *4* seems to me to resemble Lewis's *second* paradox rather than his first: Paradox *4* suppresses a necessary *premiss*, viz. (C), and not a metalogical principle. What, then, is the fundamental difference between Paradox *4* and all those other paradoxes?

In my opinion it is this. I think that *each* of those other paradoxes satisfies the following condition – which I will call (Σ) –, namely the condition that the *a priori* proof that the first premiss materially implies the conclusion assumes a premiss or principle which in an intuitive sense *obviously* entails the falsehood of the first premiss or the truth of the conclusion. In Lewis's second paradox and in the Para-doxes *1* and *3* the conclusion is in fact, in each case, identical with the suppressed premiss; in Lewis's first paradox the metalogical prin-ciple which the proof assumes *obviously* entails, in an intuitive sense, the falsehood of the first premiss. But this is not so in Paradox *4*: premiss (C) *does not obviously entail* that there are as many brothers as brothers. (And of course, the falsehood of "There are exactly ten brothers" can't be entailed by (C) at all, obviously or otherwise.) Now I think that it is only when (Σ) is satisfied that it seems intui-tively plausible to suppose that *P* does not entail *Q* because the necessity of the corresponding material implication is "based" on the modal value of *P* or the modal value of *Q*. And it is therefore only when (Σ) is satisfied that a restriction on the transitivity of entail-ment seems not to be *too* counter-intuitive to be worth consideration.

In other words, I believe that the basic intuitive idea underlying von Wright's approach would justify a restriction on transitivity only in those cases which satisfy (Σ). But if so, then Smiley's restriction is stronger than any restriction that would be justified

---

[1] They differ, however, from Lewis's second paradox in that in the special kind of case which they illustrate such premiss-suppression seems to be intuitively more justified than it does in Lewis's case.

by the basic idea of von Wright's approach. And hence, I do not think that Smiley's definition (in its generalized form) captures the basic idea which von Wright's definition tried to capture, albeit unsuccessfully.

Moreover, it seems obvious that *any* successful attempt to capture that idea *must* involve a restriction on transitivity: for so far as that idea goes, all the other moves in the proofs which we have discussed, or at least all the other moves in Lewis's *first* proof, are entirely valid.

But if this is so, then I think that the basic idea of von Wright's approach *cannot* be successfully captured. For I think that any attempt to do so will reproduce the von Wright–Smiley situation: either, like von Wright's attempt, it will fail to exclude *any* paradoxes or, like Smiley's attempt, it will disallow, by a strong restriction on transitivity, also those paradoxes in which the trouble, that is, the counter-intuitiveness of the conclusions, is *not* due to a failure of transitivity.

I will now try to put a part of what I have just said in a different way, and I will try to develop it. If we examine Paradox *4*, we find that there is *no* step with regard to which von Wright could rightly maintain that the transitivity of entailment is lost at *that* step because that step suppresses something which itself, in an intuitive sense, obviously entails that there are as many brothers as brothers. I have already pointed out that that step cannot be (C); and (II) is merely a substitution instance of (C), and hence (II) can't be that step either. Thus in order to reject (III) von Wright would have to reject (A). But (A) is all right if entailment is reflexive and adjunctive. So in order to justify the rejection of (III) von Wright would have to claim that entailment lacks one or other of those properties. But (*a*) on von Wright's definition it has those properties (certainly, it has them on Smiley's); and (*b*) in any case, if von Wright were to reject (III) by rejecting adjunction (say), then he would be acknowledging that the trouble here is not due to a failure of transitivity. Thus, his own definition of entailment does *not* allow him to reject (III).

Perhaps, however, von Wright would say that (III) is *not* paradoxical; but if so, how is he going to justify his rejection of Lewis's first paradox? So far as I can see, he can do so *only* either by abandoning his approach altogether and adopting (say) the Anderson–Belnap approach; or by abandoning his own definition, adopting Smiley's definition *for the propositional calculus*, and agreeing with me that that definition *cannot be generalized*.

But then *why* can't it be generalized? I submit that this is so for the following reason. It is only because of the relatively simple structure of the propositional calculus that Smiley's definition works in the case of Lewis's paradoxes. For, to take the first of them as an example, we can here pin-point a step, namely (δ), and say that that step suppresses something which obviously entails the denial of the first premiss; and we can then choose between Smiley's definition and say "Accept that step but restrict transitivity", and the Anderson–Belnap system and say "No, transitivity must be accepted but the step itself must be rejected". But I submit that these two methods are merely alternative (and counter-intuitive) devices which are possible in the propositional calculus, but are *not* possible in a sufficiently rich language, such as the language of my Paradox *4*.

In such a language one *cannot* get rid of conclusions which we feel are counter-intuitive, even if less so that Lewis's, either by Smiley's device or by Anderson and Belnap's.

Let us now look more closely at Paradox *4* in relation to the Anderson–Belnap approach. I have already pointed out that if one accepts step (C), one must accept step (II) since this is merely a substitution instance of (C). If, on the other hand, one rejects (C) and claims that we have to add to the antecedent of (C):

"There are exactly n ϕs and there are exactly n ψs" entails

"There are exactly as many ϕs as ψs",

then one is immediately confronted with Lewis Carroll's celebrated story of Achilles and the Tortoise.[1] Hence, I do not think that Paradox *4* can be said to involve illegitimate suppression of *any* kind. But if so, then Paradox *4* cannot be avoided on the lines of the Anderson–Belnap approach: any extension of their system which made it applicable to the Paradox (and retained unrestricted transitivity) would have to accept (III). I suppose that the theorists of the Anderson–Belnap school would claim that (III) is not *in the least* counter-intuitive.[2] But then the theorists of the Lewis school

---

[1] Lewis Carroll, "What the Tortoise said to Achilles", *Mind*, vol. 4 (1895).

[2] I also do not see how the Anderson–Belnap theorists could give a general definition of entailment which would prevent (without restricting transitivity) the derivation of the conclusion in my Paradox *1*. That is, I do not see how they could in *general* distinguish, in a language as rich as that of my Paradox *1*, between the kind of logically necessary premiss that *can* be legitimately suppressed and the kind that cannot. Yet I think they *would* regard the conclusion of Paradox *1* as unacceptable.

have claimed that *Lewis's conclusions* are not in the least counter-intuitive;[1] and *every* entailment-theorist has claimed that the results which his theory allows are not in the least counter-intuitive.[2]

What, then, do all those paradoxes really show? I now think that the right answer is as follows. Our intuitive, that is, pre-formal, concept of entailment is inconsistent.[3] We wish to accept all the steps in, e.g., Lewis's first proof; and we wish to accept the un-restricted transitivity of entailment; if we accept all this, we must, of course, accept Lewis's conclusion; but *this* we don't wish to accept. We feel that there *must be* "something wrong" with the proof.

Those who accept Lewis's definition as a correct *analysis* of the intuitive concept of entailment must hold that Lewis's conclusions are not *at all* counter-intuitive but merely surprising.

I think there are good (although not conclusive) inductive reasons against this. In normal mathematical cases, when a con-clusion of a proof is surprising, the proof is long and complex or involves a new or unfamiliar technique. But Lewis's proofs are very short and simple and involve no new or unfamiliar technique. In view of this, I think it is unlikely that all the numerous philosophers and logicians who rejected Lewis's conclusions have been as thoroughly confused as the assumption that those conclusions are merely surprising requires us to suppose. This is possible, but I think unlikely. It should also be remembered in this connexion that those opponents of Lewis's did not all share the same philo-sophical background. And they included G. E. Moore, C. D. Broad, John Wisdom, E. J. Nelson, A. E. Duncan-Jones, W. T. Parry, P. F. Strawson, G. H. von Wright, P. T. Geach, W. Ackermann, A. R. Anderson, D. N. Belnap and many others. Also, as I have already mentioned, Lewis himself at first rejected the paradoxes.[4]

I do not wish, however, to rest my case merely on this inductive evi-dence, and I think I can perhaps bring other arguments in its support.

---

[1] Anderson and Belnap (*op. cit.* p. 18), on the other hand, say that they agree with those who find Lewis's first proof *self-evidently preposterous*!

[2] Downing, for instance, would claim that "Caesar is dead ≡ this has shape" entails "This has shape ≡ this has size", but that $(P \& \sim P)$ does *not* entail Q, and that the conjunction of (A) and (C) in my Paradox *1* does *not* entail (B).

[3] I already expressed this opinion in my lectures in the Easter Term of 1964, although I was then still uncertain as to what would be the best reconstruction of the concept.

[4] I have not so far mentioned Broad or Duncan-Jones. The relevant sources are: C. D. Broad, *Examination of McTaggart's Philosophy*, vol. 1 (Cambridge, 1934), Ch. XI; A. E. Duncan-Jones, "Is Strict Implication the same as Entailment?", *Analysis*, vol. 2 (1934–5). Duncan-Jones's approach is very similar to Nelson's,

Let us restrict ourselves for the moment to the propositional calculus, and let us call the relation defined by Smiley *S*-necessitation. Now consider the following three propositions:

(1) *S*-necessitation is a sufficient condition for "*P* entails *Q*";
(2) Entailment is unrestrictedly transitive;
(3) It is not the case that (*P* & ~ *P*) entails *Q*.

This triad is patently inconsistent; yet we feel a strong inclination to accept *all* the three propositions. Is this due to sheer confusion? I think that if we put the matter in this way, the answer almost forces itself upon us that this is *not* so: that each proposition brings out an intuition which we have in this area, but that these intuitions are inconsistent, so that *no* relation can satisfy all of them.

And consider now how, in effect, the different theorists we have been discussing reacted to the triad: Anderson and Belnap, Nelson, Parry, Strawson, all gave up (1), although for different reasons;[1] von Wright and Geach gave up (2); Lewis gave up (3). I myself thought for some years that we should distinguish between *two* concepts of entailment, one of which satisfies (2) but not (1), and the other of which satisfies (1) but not (2).

I now think that all these "solutions" are in fact alternative reconstructions of an inconsistent concept. Clearly, Lewis's theory is the *simplest* reconstruction; but I now think that it is also much the best because, for sufficiently rich languages, there is in any case no theory of entailment, however complex, which would enable

except for a difference which I need not go into. The case of Broad is interesting. His reference to Nelson in the Preface to the book may suggest that in his discussion of entailment he is following Nelson's approach; but in fact I think the position is more complicated. I think that Broad fails to distinguish between the Nelson and the von Wright types of approach, but that he is predominantly following, that is, historically speaking, anticipating, the latter.

The von Wright approach seems to have been influenced by some ideas of W. E. Johnson's. (Cf. W. E. Johnson, *Logic*, Pt. I (Cambridge, 1921), Ch. III, Secs. 7 and 8, esp. pp. 42–3.) In fact, in Broad's case Johnson's influence is quite clear. The relevant paragraphs of Johnson's book are considered at some length in von Wright's paper, and they are also mentioned briefly in Smiley's. I do not wish to discuss Johnson's ideas in detail, but I will say this. I do not think that Johnson himself would have adopted von Wright's approach. In my opinion, Johnson would have claimed that the "paradoxes" of strict implication are true of entailment but that they are harmless. I think that careful reading of his, admittedly rather obscure, text does not leave much doubt on this point. I believe Broad's discussion is in effect the first attempt, at any rate in print, to extract from Johnson's ideas a definition of entailment which would avoid the "paradoxes".

[1] Nelson's case is really more complicated since he does need a restriction on transitivity as well; but this is not important in the present connexion.

us to accept all those entailment propositions which on an intuitive level we wish to accept and reject all those which on an intuitive level we wish to reject. And, so far as I can see, there is no *hope* of such a theory. Finally, but perhaps most importantly, I now think that the consequences of accepting Lewis's theory are *less* counter-intuitive than the consequences of accepting any of the alternative theories. In particular, to take the two theories to which we have devoted most of our attention, I think it is less counter-intuitive to accept that $(P \mathbin{\&} \sim P)$ entails Q than to reject the principle that $[\sim P \mathbin{\&} (P \lor Q)]$ entails Q; and that it is less counter-intuitive to accept the former than to reject the unrestricted transitivity of entailment. In view of all this, it seems to me that much the best course is to accept (1) and (2) of our inconsistent triad, each of which in any case accords with a strong inclination we have in this area, and *suppress* that inclination, even if we feel it strongly too, which makes us accept (3). This is a rectification of an inconsistent concept, but I think it is the most rational one.

There is, however, another important matter which we must discuss in this connexion. What is the *source* of the conflicting inclinations which we have in this area? I think the answer is as follows. In our everyday thinking we *normally* infer a contingent conclusion from premises which (taken together) are also contingent, although we do *sometimes* infer a conclusion from premises which (taken together) are inconsistent. Let us express this briefly by saying that we normally restrict ourselves in our inferences to contingent propositions. But at a certain stage we wish to extend the relation of entailment to the class of *all* propositions. And this is not just for the sake of producing a unified theory, important though it is to have such a theory: the extension is required by a strong intuition that it must *not* be the case that in the absence of a proof of the consistency of the premises in an argument, every single step in it may have to be retracted.[1] Indeed, it is this which makes any attempt to restrict entailment to contingent propositions so strongly counter-intuitive.[2] But if we do make this very com-

---

[1] See Smiley, *op. cit.* p. 224. It may also be worth mentioning that the counter-intuitive nature of restricting entailment to contingent propositions is well brought out by my Paradox *1*: for the restriction would have the consequence that the conjunction of (A) and (C) does not entail (B).

[2] There are other troubles about restricting entailment to contingent propositions, some of which I will mention in Chapter 10. But they are not important at this point.

pelling extension, our troubles begin: principles which led to no difficulties when we restricted ourselves to contingent propositions, now do lead to difficulties. Clearly, we must now make a *decision* as to how to deal with the matter; and as I have said, the best decision is to identify entailment with strict implication.

To put a part of the above in a different way. I do not think that the inconsistency of the intuitive concept of entailment is due *primarily* to the conflict between our desire to preserve unrestricted transitivity and our desire to allow the suppression of necessarily true premisses and principles in certain kinds of case, although this is an important aspect of the matter.[1] I think that Paradox *4* shows that even in cases where "illegitimate suppression" is not involved, and hence a restriction on transitivity has no intuitive justification, we still feel that certain conclusions are paradoxical: but in those cases we feel that they are *less* paradoxical than in the cases which do involve the conflict just mentioned.

3

I shall now discuss a few related points.

J. F. Bennett,[2] who seems to think that the intuitive concept of entailment is consistent, says that Smiley's non-transitive entailment (which he calls S-entailment) is in effect a formalized version of "one-step" entailment (p. 210). Or at least this is what he asserts in *one* passage; in another passage, on the very same page, he seems to qualify this by saying:

> It [S-entailment] does *perhaps*[3] reconstruct the idea of intuitive entailment – that is, of obvious or elementary or one-step entailment; but that is not what has to be shown.[4]

[1] This of course is the aspect which my Paradoxes *1* and *2* (disregarding the connexion of the latter with propositional identity) of the 1958 paper brought out, I *believe* for the first time. But my suggested solution of them by distinguishing two senses of "entails" was wrong; and my further attempt (though advanced very tentatively) to explain these alleged two senses was *completely* unsuccessful. It is easy to see one's confusions after the lapse of some years; it is very difficult to do so when one is struck by a new aspect of a problem.

[2] J. F. Bennett, "Entailment", *The Philosophical Review*, vol. 78 (1969).

[3] The italics are mine.

[4] I.e. that is not what has to be shown in order to show that S-entailment is a satisfactory reconstruction of the intuitive idea of entailment.

So far as I can see, the word "elementary" is introduced in the above passage for the first time and without any further explanation.

But surely to suppose that Smiley's criterion reconstructs the idea of *obvious* entailment is a complete mistake, and this for two separate reasons. First, consider:

$$(A) \quad (P \supset Q) \supset \{[(P \supset R) \supset S] \supset [(Q \supset R) \supset S]\}.$$

This expresses a tautology which satisfies Smiley's criterion. But is it *obvious* that the antecedent of (A) entails its consequent? Perhaps it is to Bennett, but surely not to everybody. And of course there are far more complicated formulae than (A) which also satisfy Smiley's criterion. It is *absurd* to suppose that to every tautology which has the implication sign as the main connective and which satisfies Smiley's criterion, there corresponds an *obvious* entailment proposition. Such tautologies may be miles long.

Secondly, as Smiley himself points out (p. 240), transitivity does hold for "*S*-entailment" when the original premisses (taken together) and the final conclusion are contingent propositions. But clearly, this is *not* true of obvious entailment. It follows immediately that the two are different.

I suppose, however, that it is *just* possible that Bennett wished to make some distinction between "obvious entailment" and "one-step entailment", although the sentence which I have quoted from him hardly admits of such construction.

But if so (and to be fair to him, I do not really think that it is so), then how has he defined "one-step entailment"? All that he says on the point is this (p. 210):

> Let us call a principle of inference "basic" if one application of it can lead from a contingent premise to a contingent conclusion: then "*P* *S*-entails *Q*" can be defined as "*Q* can be derived from *P* by a single application of a basic principle of inference". This validates every step in the Lewis argument,[1] but does not validate the move from $(P \& \sim P)$ to Q.

But what has Bennett done here? Why, he has merely reformulated, in a less clear way, Smiley's criterion. And he has obscured the fact that a "basic" principle of inference, in this sense, may be fantastically complicated: he has obscured the fact that Smiley's criterion involves a reference to the notion of a substitution instance.

As I have said, however, I do not really think that Bennett wished

---

[1] I.e. in Lewis's first proof.

to distinguish between "obvious entailment" and "one-step entailment". I think it is fairly clear that he used these two expressions
synonymously, and thought that "*S*-entailment" reconstructs, or
that it *perhaps* reconstructs, the idea which we express when we say
that *P* obviously entails *Q*. And this, as I have shown, is a complete mistake.

I have not gone into all this just in order to show that Bennett
has made a mistake; I have done so for a much more important
reason. I think it is by no means an accident that he wanted to
claim that Smiley's criterion reconstructs *some* intuitive idea. Why?
Because there is something very compelling about the criterion: we
all have the feeling that it does "capture" *some* intuitive concept. But
what intuitive concept? Certainly, it is not that of obvious entailment; and although I cannot be certain that somebody will not
succeed in pointing out such a concept, I submit that the criterion
"captures" *no* intuitive concept. It merely accords, but only in the
special case of the propositional calculus, with those intuitions which
make us want to accept every step in Lewis's first proof and also
make us want to reject his final conclusion, but which conflict with
our intuition that entailment is transitive.

I think these considerations – that there is something very compelling about Smiley's criterion and that yet there seems to be no
intuitive concept which the criterion "captures" – lend additional
support to my claim that the intuitive concept of entailment is
inconsistent.

I have one further point to make in this connexion. J. L. Pollock,
in an able paper, suggests in effect that I confused entailment with
the relation which he expresses by the words "part of what it means
to say that... is that – – –".[1] He says that my paradoxes *1* and *2* of
the 1958 paper show that we have *two* implicative relations to
contend with – entailment and the relation just mentioned; and he
holds that the respective conclusions of those two paradoxes are
acceptable for entailment, but are not acceptable for the other
relation.

I cannot discuss Pollock's paper in detail.[2] But I will say this.
Although I have been guilty of plenty of confusions in this area, I

[1] John L. Pollock, "The Paradoxes of Strict Implication", *Logique et Analyse*, vol 9
(1966), p. 191.
[2] In any case, the paper only came to my notice after I had already arrived, in all
essential respects, at the views expressed in this Chapter.

do not think that I have been guilty of this particular confusion. For as Pollock himself points out (p. 191), the relation which he expresses by the words "part of what it means to say that... is that – – –" is meant to give us those implications "which can be known immediately, without proof", that is, as I think we can also put it, *obvious* logical implications, i.e. *obvious* entailments. And I do not think that I have ever confused entailment with *obvious entailment*.

I also do not think that the relation of obvious entailment can properly be expressed by Pollock's phrase "part of what it means to say that... is that – – –". I think that *this* phrase expresses rather the relation which in the last Chapter I called "analytic entailment". And it is entirely clear that I could not have confused *this* relation with entailment. I could not have confused it with my "necessitation" of the 1958 paper since that was expressly meant *not* to be unrestrictedly transitive whereas I have always thought that "analytic entailment" *is* unrestrictedly transitive. And I could not have confused it with my transitive entailment of the 1958 paper since I have never thought that "analytic entailment" is a necessary condition for entailment in the pre-formal, intuitive sense of "entails".

My reason for thinking that "*P* obviously entails *Q*" cannot properly be expressed by Pollock's phrase "part of what it means to say that... is that – – –" is as follows. I think it is true that "John is a brother" obviously entails "John is a brother ∨ London is larger than Cambridge"; I do *not* think it is true that part of what it means to say that John is a brother is that John is a brother ∨ London is larger than Cambridge. I also think it is true that "This is red" obviously entails "This is coloured"; I do *not* think that part of what it means to say that this is red is that this is coloured. And similarly, I think that "This has shape" obviously entails and is obviously entailed by "This has size"; I do *not* think that part of what is meant by saying that this has shape is that this has size or that part of what is meant by saying that this has size is that this has shape.

In other words, I think that Pollock has failed to distinguish between two quite different relations, namely obvious entailment which is *not* transitive and analytic entailment which *is* transitive.[1]

[1] I think that synthetic entailment, as defined in Chapter 8, is also unrestrictedly transitive; but of course I do not identify synthetic entailment with obvious

In any case, Pollock's second implicative relation does not give us any intuitive concept which can be said to be captured by *Smiley's criterion* – for as I have shown Smiley's criterion does not capture *obvious* entailment. And I think that Pollock may well agree with me on *this* since, so far as I can see, Pollock does not make the mistake that Bennett has made: Pollock does not think, so far as I can see, that a proposition which requires a proof using the rule of substitution, requires no proof!

There is another comment that I wish to make on Bennett's paper.

I said earlier that Bennett *seems to think* that the intuitive concept of entailment is consistent, rather than that he *thinks* that this is so. I have done so because his discussion of this matter is not entirely clear to me. In particular, on his very first page,[1] after stating that Lewis maintained that to say that P entails Q is to say that it is logically impossible that $(P \& \sim Q)$, and after making a few remarks (not really relevant to the subject) about the alleged suspectedness of intensional terms in general, he continues:

> I shall argue that Lewis was right, and also – by implication – that his thesis is helpful and clarifying – that is, that it is a genuine analysis.

But now, as Bennett has stated the matter, there is simply *no* difference between supposing that *Lewis is right* and supposing that *Lewis's "thesis" is right*. Hence if Lewis is right, as Bennett thinks he is, it follows immediately that Lewis's "thesis" is right – that is, it follows immediately that the assertion "P entails Q" is *identical* with the assertion "It is logically impossible that $(P \& \sim Q)$".

But if so, what is one really to make of Bennett's statement? Why does he say that he will argue, and this only by implication, that Lewis's "thesis" is *helpful and clarifying*? And why does he here identify, as he expressly does, "being a genuine analysis" with "being helpful and clarifying"?

To put it bluntly: Why doesn't Bennett simply say, as he ought to say if he thinks that Lewis is right, that Lewis's definition is a correct analysis of the intuitive concept of entailment? I do not

---

entailment. In my opinion, some analytic entailments are obvious whilst others are not; and some synthetic entailments are obvious whilst others are not.

[1] *Op. cit.* p. 197.

know, but I think the answer is as follows. On the one hand, Bennett cannot bring himself to say plainly that the intuitive concept of entailment is consistent, and that Lewis has given a correct analysis of it. On the other hand, he also cannot bring himself to say plainly that the concept is *in*consistent, but that Lewis has given the best "rational reconstruction" of it.

Bennett's concluding section (pp. 235–6), and the general tone of his paper, suggest that he holds the former view; the circumlocution of the statement I have quoted from him appears to suggest a conflict.

Moreover, when in his Section VII he comes to discuss explicitly whether the intuitive concept of entailment is inconsistent, he still fails to give a definite answer.

This is what he says (p. 212):

> *Is* the common concept of entailment inconsistent? Those who accept each step in the Lewis argument, and agree that entailment is transitive, yet deny the paradox, are indeed guilty of inconsistency; but that is a fact about them rather than about entailment. The fact that many people, while accepting each step in the Lewis argument, and so forth, are strongly inclined to deny the paradox, may look more like evidence for inconsistency in the concept; though even here less charitable diagnoses are possible. But if it is clear that we ought to accept the paradox, it does not matter much whether this acceptance is described as our rectifying a previously inconsistent concept or as our handling more competently the consistent concept we have had all along.

I think however that this does matter, and matters very much. Partly because if the "common concept" is inconsistent, then the reaction of Lewis's opponents was altogether less discreditable – in fact, if it was discreditable at all, it was not so in the same way – than it would have been had Lewis really discovered a correct analysis of a "common concept". And partly because the latter description importantly misrepresents the nature of what Lewis has done.

Finally, Bennett seems to attribute to Smiley the view that "ordinary transitive entailment" is the ancestral of "*S*-entailment" (p. 210). I can see nothing in Smiley's paper which really warrants this attribution; but I don't wish to go into a minute analysis of Smiley's paper on this matter. Bennett adds, in parentheses, that if "ordinary entailment" were not transitive, it could not be the ancestral of anything. This is entirely right: the ancestral of a relation R is always transitive, even if R itself is not transitive.

I should myself put the point which is here at issue as follows. Whatever the correct definition of "obviously entails" may be, to define "entails" so that it is *not* the ancestral of "obviously entails" is strongly counter-intuitive.

We must notice, however, that the various relations which we have ben discussing, e.g. the Anderson–Belnap relation, Smiley's relation, etc., are all *implication relations which hold on purely logical grounds*. (They are of course narrower than strict implication.) Hence, in a wide sense of the term, they may be called "entailment relations". I think that although they are not acceptable as reconstructions of our pre-formal, intuitive concept of entailment, the investigation of their properties is an interesting and worthwhile undertaking.

4

I shall now discuss von Wright's definition of entailment. As I have already mentioned, the definition[1] is as follows:

P entails Q, if and only if, by means of logic, it is possible to come to know the truth of $P \supset Q$ without coming to know the falsehood of P or the truth of Q.[2]

I wish to make the following comments on this definition.

1. It seems at least uncertain whether this will be of any use at all for the following reason. Von Wright assumes that if it is possible to come to know that P materially implies Q, then P materially implies Q. Unless this is so, his definition won't even secure that P does materially imply Q!

I should have thought, however, that, in general, from "It is logically possible to come to know that P is true", it only follows that it is logically possible that P is true, *not* that P is true. So von Wright can't mean by "possible" logically possible. What, then, does he mean? He asserts that there is *a* sense of "possible" in which if P is false, then it is *not* possible that P should be known to be true[3] – where this does not mean of course that it is not possible

---

1 Geach calls it a "truth-condition"; I will continue to refer to it as a "definition", using here these two terms synonymously, as I have already done in connexion with Smiley's definition.

2 *Op. cit.* p. 181. I have slightly altered von Wright's symbolism.

3 *Op. cit.* pp. 183–4 and p. 183n.

that *P* should be false and yet known to be true (which is obvious). But he gives no reason whatever for his assertion. And I don't believe that it is true.

2. Let us however overlook this, and let us suppose that his definition is equivalent to:

P entails *Q* if and only if

(1) $\sim \Diamond \sim (P \supset Q)$

and

(2)   It is possible to come to know that $P \supset Q$, without coming to know the falsehood of *P* or the truth of *Q*.

How does von Wright propose to get rid of Lewis's first independent proof? The odd thing is that he does not discuss this proof.

But consider:

(1) $P \,\&\, \sim P$
(2) P
(3) $\sim P$
(4) $P \vee Q$
(5) Q.

Von Wright's entailment (I will call it *W*-entailment and symbolize it by "*W*-ent") is such that he *must* accept that $(P \,\&\, \sim P)$ *W*-ent *P* and that $(P \,\&\, \sim P)$ *W*-ent $\sim P$, and hence also the step from (1) to (2), and that from (1) to (3). Also, he *must* accept that *P* *W*-ent $(P \vee Q)$, and hence also the step from (2) to (4). Similarly, he *must* accept that $[\sim P \,\&\, (P \vee Q)]$ *W*-ent *Q*, and hence also the step from (3) and (4) to (5).

All this is so because it is possible, with respect to *each* of the material implications which are involved, to "come to know" *its* truth without "coming to know" the falsity of *its* antecedent or the truth of *its* consequent.

Hence, if von Wright is to get rid of the conclusion of Lewis's first proof, he must reject the transitivity of entailment. And another *very* odd thing is that he nowhere mentions in the course of his paper that his entailment is not transitive! Surely, this is such an important feature (and *prima facie* at least, such a *highly* counter-intuitive feature) of his entailment relation that he should have mentioned it.[1]

---

[1] Von Wright agreed in discussions with me some time between 1959 and 1961 that his entailment is not unrestrictedly transitive.

3. I will now show *conclusively* that von Wright's definition (which is of course quite general and is not restricted to the calculus of propositions) won't do at all.

Consider the following passage from von Wright's paper:[1]

> The following is a law of modal logic: Nq & $N(p$ & $q \to r) \to N(p \to r)$. It is sometimes rendered in words, rather inaccurately, by saying that 'a necessary premiss may be omitted'.
>
> Now suppose that we had established the necessity of the material implication p & $q \to r$ independently of its antecedent and consequent. This means that the conjunction p & q entails r, on my definition of entailment. Suppose further that we have also established the necessity of q. It then follows from the above law of modal logic that we have also established the necessity of the material implication $p \to r$. And since we have established it without either proving or disproving its antecedent and consequent, we shall also have to say that, on my definition, p entails r. All this is in good order.[2]

I fear that all this is *very far* from being in good order.

For consider the following case.

Take for Q: $1 + 1 = 2$, and for R: $(1 + 1) + 1 = (2 + 1)$. The necessity of:

$$(1 + 1 = 2) \supset [(1 + 1) + 1 = (2 + 1)]$$

can be established of course without proving that

$$\sim (1 + 1 = 2)$$

or that

$$(1 + 1) + 1 = (2 + 1).$$

Hence,

(A) $(1 + 1 = 2)$ W-ent $[(1 + 1) + 1 = (2 + 1)]$.

But now take for P: Caesar is dead. Clearly, if Q W-ent R, then $(P$ & $Q)$ W-ent R.

Hence,

(B)   [C. is dead & $(1 + 1 = 2)$] W-ent $[(1 + 1) + 1 = (2 + 1)]$.

---

[1] *Op. cit.* pp. 188–9. In this passage von Wright uses "N" for "$\sim \Diamond \sim$" and "$\to$" for "$\supset$".

[2] In our notation the "law of modal logic" to which von Wright refers is of course:

$$\{\sim \Diamond \sim Q \ \& \sim \Diamond \sim [(P \ \& \ Q) \supset R]\} \supset \sim \Diamond \sim (P \supset R)$$

which is equivalent to:

$$\{\sim \Diamond \sim Q \ \& \ [(P \ \& \ Q) \to R]\} \supset (P \to R).$$

I have myself referred to it in this work several times.

But

    (C) $\sim \Diamond \sim (1+1 = 2)$.

Hence ("by the above law of modal logic"),

    (D)   (C. is dead) $\dashv3\,[(1+1)+1 = (2+1)]$.

And of course (D) is true. However, since we have established (D) without either proving its consequent or disproving its antecedent, "we shall have to say" that

    (E)   (C. is dead) W-ent $[(1+1)+1 = (2+1)]$.

Reductio ad absurdum. ("All this" was *not* in good order!)

Can von Wright escape my *reductio* by saying that in "coming to know" (C), i.e. in "coming to know" that "$1+1 = 2$" is necessary, we would be "coming to know" that "$(1+1)+1 = (2+1)$" is necessary (and thus would also be "coming to know" that $(1+1)+1 = (2+1)$)?

No, such a claim would be obviously false: knowledge is not transitive over entailment.

Let me put it more fully, even if a little tediously. The conjunction of:

    (1) $(1+1 = 2)$ entails[1] $[(1+1)+1 = (2+1)]$;

    (2) $\sim \Diamond \sim (1+1 = 2)$;

and

    (3)   Whatever is entailed by a necessary proposition is itself necessary[2]

entails:

    (4) $\sim \Diamond \sim [(1+1)+1 = (2+1)]$.

And of course (4) entails:

    (5) $(1+1)+1 = (2+1)$.

But firstly, it just isn't true that anybody who knows (1) and (2) must also know (3). And secondly, even if a man does know (1), (2) *and* (3), he need not know (4): it is simply false that if P entails Q and A knows that P is true, then A knows that Q is true. And thirdly (and for the same reason), even if a man does know (4), he need not know (5) (however unlikely the last possibility may be in practice).

No, there is simply *no* escape for von Wright.

4. But now, von Wright may say: Yes, you have certainly shown

---

[1] Both in the sense of "$\dashv3$" and in the sense of von Wright (of course my point is that the two are identical).

[2] That is, using "$\dashv3$" for "entails":

$$[(P \dashv3 Q)\ \&\ \sim \Diamond \sim P] \supset\ \sim \Diamond \sim Q.$$

that my definition, which, as you have pointed out, is completely general and is not restricted to the calculus of propositions, simply fails to distinguish between entailment and strict implication. But if we do restrict its applicability to the calculus of propositions, then in this restricted field it *will* work.[1] In particular, it will get rid of Lewis's first proof by rejecting the unrestricted transitivity of entailment – for, as you have rightly pointed out, it *must* do this to get rid of it.

But this won't do: von Wright's definition does *not* restrict transitivity in a way which is required to avoid the conclusion of Lewis's first proof.[2]

It would be very tedious to discuss this really exhaustively. But I will make the following remarks.

It is clear that von Wright would have to claim that at *some* step in Lewis's first proof (at least at *one* step, but possibly at more than one), the material implication which corresponds to it is such that it is impossible "to come to know" its truth without "coming to know" that it is *not* the case that (P & $\sim P$) or that it *is* the case that Q. Now since we are discussing Lewis's *first* proof, the latter alternative can be left out. So von Wright's claim would come to this: that at *some* step in Lewis's proof, the material implication which corresponds to it is such that it is impossible to "come to know" its truth without "coming to know" that it is not the case that (P & $\sim P$).

But at *which* step, or steps, is this so? Clearly, at *no* step. For at whatever step von Wright alleged this to be so, the argument of § 3 could be used against him.

5. In a later paper von Wright says that he thinks there is a sense in which a truth-table demonstration of (A) $P \supset (\sim P \supset Q)$ is not independent of a proof of the falsity of (P & $\sim P$).[3]

Is this true also of (A') $P \supset (P \vee Q)$? I can't see how *this* could be supported at all. Yet in two-valued logic "$P \vee Q$" is merely another way of writing "$\sim P \supset Q$". All I need to do therefore is to rewrite (A) as (A'); and then I can give a truth-table

1 This is in effect what von Wright did say when in a discussion with him some time between 1959 and 1961 I informed him of the proof given in § 3.
2 As J. F. Bennett accurately reports, I made this point in 1958 at Southampton in the discussion following the symposium on entailment (and also mentioned that this is the position with respect to Lewis's second proof as well). See J. F. Bennett, "On a Recent Account of Entailment", *Mind*, vol. 68 (1959), esp. the footnote on p. 394.
3 G. H. von Wright, "A Note on Entailment", *Philosophical Quarterly*, vol. 9 (1959), p. 365. This is a reply to Strawson's review of *Logical Studies* in vol. 8 (1958).

demonstration of (A′) – a demonstration which is quite independent of a demonstration of the falsity of (P & $\sim P$).

Let me develop this.

Is von Wright suggesting that although the step from (2) to (4) in Lewis's first proof is valid, it is the material implication corresponding to it which is such that it is impossible to "come to know its truth" without "coming to know" the falsity of (P & $\sim P$)? Let us call a material implication having this property an "offending" implication. Is then, according to von Wright, the offending implication involved in Lewis's first proof:

(A′) $P \supset (P \vee Q)$?

But as I have just said this allegation seems quite unsupportable.

What then is the explanation of all this? I can only suggest the following answer.

In his 1959 paper von Wright still does not discuss Lewis's first proof in the standard form that I have given. Instead, he imagines that a supporter of the view that (P & $\sim P$) entails Q, produces the following proof. (Let us call it proof (α).)

(A) $P \supset (\sim P \supset Q)$.
(B) $[P \supset (R \supset Q)] \supset [(P \& R) \supset Q]$.

In (B) substitute $\sim P$ for R:

This give us (by the rule of substitution)

(C) $[P \supset (\sim P \supset Q)] \supset [(P \& \sim P) \supset Q]$.

From (A) and (C), by *modus ponens*, we get:

(D) $(P \& \sim P) \supset Q$.

Now von Wright claims that the offending implication here is (A). But in the standard form of the proof the offending implication *cannot* be (A′); yet (A) and (A′) are absolutely synonymous! Surely this is absurd.

And what is the offending implication, according to von Wright, in this proof? (Let us call it proof (β).)

(1) $P \supset (P \vee Q)$.
(2) $[P \supset (R \supset Q)] \supset [(P \& R) \supset Q]$.

In (2) substitute $\sim P$ for R:

(3) $[P \supset (\sim P \supset Q)] \supset [(P \& \sim P) \supset Q]$.
(4) $P \vee Q \underset{\text{df}}{=} \sim P \supset Q$.

By the rule of definitional replacement we get:

(5) $[P \supset (P \vee Q)] \supset [(P \& \sim P) \supset Q]$.

From (1) and (5), by *modus ponens*, we get:

(6) $(P \& \sim P) \supset Q$.

Surely, according to von Wright, there can be *no* offending implication here.

Hence, even if von Wright can get rid of *his* form of the proof by making (A) the culprit, and of the standard form of the proof by making

$$[\sim P \,\&\, (P \vee Q)] \supset Q$$

the culprit (of course, he can't do either, as I have already pointed out), he still has $(P \,\&\, \sim P)$ *W*-ent Q!

What, then, is wrong with von Wright's 1959 treatment of the problem? I think it is this. Von Wright has failed to see that the only plausible candidate for the offending implication in his proof (α) is *not* (A), which he says it is, but (B), which he explicitly says it isn't!

For it is (B) which is not, of course, a three-valued tautology; both (A) and (A') *are* three-valued tautologies. So the only *prima facie* sensible course to take would be to put the blame on $[\sim P \,\&\, (P \vee Q)] \supset Q$ in the standard form of Lewis's first proof, and on (B) in proofs (α) and (β). But of course this wouldn't help von Wright in the end. For (1) to each of these two implications there corresponds a true *W*-entailment proposition, and (2) it isn't the case that the knowledge of either of these two implications entails the knowledge of the falsity of $(P \,\&\, \sim P)$ – unless we make the plainly false assumption that if P entails Q and A knows that P is true, than A knows that Q is true.

So von Wright would still in the end get the conclusion that $(P \,\&\, \sim P)$ *W*-ent Q. He has *not* restricted the transitivity of his entailment in a way which would be required to avoid Lewis's first paradox.

And if so, then he has not avoided Lewis's second paradox either: for this can be derived from the first paradox by contraposition.

I will now summarize briefly the main part of this Section. Von Wright has failed to see that Lewis's first proof assumes the principle of bivalence, and does not involve the suppression of a necessarily true *premiss*; he has so defined entailment that to the material implication which involves this assumption, i.e. to $[\sim P \,\&\, (P \vee Q)] \supset Q$, there corresponds a true entailment proposition, and hence the course taken by Anderson and Belnap was not open to him; he thought that by restricting the transitivity of entailment he has avoided the paradox; but he has failed to notice that the above material implication, to which on his definition of entailment this loss of transitivity must be attributed, does not satisfy the condition which it would have to satisfy in order that his definition should avoid the paradox – knowledge of that material implication does *not* entail knowledge of the falsity of $(P \& \sim P)$.

Addendum. Perhaps I should explain, for the sake of those who are not very familiar with Łukasiewicz's (1921) three-valued logic, the position with regard to (B).

In two-valued logic we have of course:
$$[P \supset (Q \supset R)] \equiv [(P \& Q) \supset R];$$
but in three-valued logic the following is *not* a theorem (i.e. it is not a "three-valued tautology"):
$$[P \supset (Q \supset R)] \supset [(P \& Q) \supset R],$$
although the following *is* a theorem:
$$[(P \& Q) \supset R] \supset [P \supset (Q \supset R)].$$

Of course the *rule* of *modus ponens* (or detachment, as it is sometimes called) that is, the rule "From α and $\alpha \supset \beta$ infer β", can be used in three-valued logic. But the well-formed formula, sometimes also called *modus ponens*, i.e. the formula "$[P \& (P \supset Q)] \supset Q$", is not a theorem. On the other hand, the purely implicational form of it[1] *is* a theorem.

[1] I.e. $P \supset [(P \supset Q) \supset Q]$.

IO

Entailment: II

I will now consider certain further problems about entailment.

Let us say that P is truth-functionally equivalent to Q if and only if $P \equiv Q$ is a substitution instance of $P' \equiv Q'$ such that (*a*) $P' \equiv Q'$ is a tautology,[1] and (*b*) no proper well-formed part of $P' \equiv Q'$ is a tautology.

Example.

    (1) $P \& (Q \lor \sim Q)$;
    (2) $(P \& Q) \lor (P \& \sim Q)$.

Here (1) is truth-functionally equivalent to (2) since

    (1) $\equiv$ (2)

is a substitution instance of a tautology which satisfies conditions (*a*) and (*b*), namely, the tautology:

    (A) $[P \& (Q \lor R)] \equiv [(P \& Q) \lor (P \& R)]$.[2]

If we call tautologies, such as (A), which satisfy (*a*) and (*b*) "non-redundant" tautologies, we can say that P is truth-functionally equivalent to Q if and only if $P \equiv Q$ is a substitution instance of a non-redundant tautology.

On the other hand, consider:

    (3) P;
    (4) $P \& (Q \lor \sim Q)$.

Here (3) is *not* truth-functionally equivalent to (4) since

    $P \equiv [P \& (Q \lor \sim Q)]$,

although of course a tautology, is not a substitution instance of a non-redundant tautology.

Next, let us say that P is *purely* contingent if and only if

    (1) P is contingent,
    (2)   There is no Q such that (*a*) Q contains a tautologous conjunct, and (*b*) Q is truth-functionally equivalent to P.[3]

---

[1] By a tautology I shall always mean a tautology of the two-valued propositional calculus.

[2] For the sake of simplicity I use capital letters throughout.

[3] This notion of a "purely" contingent proposition was introduced (in a more general form) in my 1958 paper.

Now consider the following definition (or truth-condition):[1]

$P \twoheadrightarrow Q$ if and only if $P \supset Q$ is a substitution instance of $P' \supset Q'$ such that

(1) $P' \supset Q'$ is a tautology,

(2) Q' is purely contingent,

(3) $\sim P'$ is purely contingent.

This of course defines "$\twoheadrightarrow$" for the propositional calculus only.

I shall read "$\twoheadrightarrow$" as "strictly entails", and I wish to make some remarks about this notion and about certain related matters.

1. I conjecture that "$\twoheadrightarrow$" is unrestrictedly transitive; but I don't know how to prove it.

2. I conjecture (but cannot prove) that the implication relation of Anderson and Belnap satisfies my definition of "$\twoheadrightarrow$".[2]

3. If this last conjecture is right, then what Anderson and Belnap have done is, I think, this. They have succeeded in constructing, *for the propositional calculus*, a relation of logical implication which forbids *both* "premiss suppression" (which occurs in Lewis's second "independent" proof) *and* "principle suppression" (which occurs in his first "independent" proof).

Of course they have to give up:

$[\sim P \& (P \lor Q)]$ entails Q.

(That is, they have to maintain that to the tautology which is usually called the law of disjunctive syllogism – viz. $[\sim P \& (P \lor Q)] \supset Q$ – there does not correspond a true entailment proposition.)

This, as I have already stressed, is strongly counter-intuitive.

4. Moreover, I do not see how my definition of "$\twoheadrightarrow$" could be generalized beyond the propositional calculus – my Paradox *4* seems to show that the undertaking cannot be carried through.

I will return to some aspects of points (3) and (4) later.

5. Let us now recall Smiley's definition of what I have called *S*-necessitation:

P *S*-necessitates Q if and only if $P \supset Q$ is a substitution instance of $P' \supset Q'$ such that

---

[1] I first formulated it in my lectures in the academic year 1961–62.

[2] I first made these two conjectures in June 1966. They were included in my lectures at the University of Texas at Austin in the autumn semester of 1967–68.

(1) $P' \supset Q'$ is a tautology,

(2) Q' is contingent,

(3) P' is contingent.

Conditions (1), (2) and (3), taken together, are equivalent to Smiley's set which has, instead of (2), "It is not the case that Q' is a tautology" and, instead of (3), "It is not the case that $\sim P'$ is a tautology".

Consider now the following definition:

$$P \overset{n}{\twoheadrightarrow} Q \text{ if and only if } P \supset Q \text{ is a substitution instance of }$$
$P' \supset Q'$ such that

(1') $P' \supset Q'$ is a tautology,

(2') Q' is purely contingent,

(3') P' is contingent.

Let us read "$\overset{n}{\twoheadrightarrow}$" as "strictly necessitates".

This relation, suggested in effect in my 1958 paper, is not only non-transitive; it is also non-contrapositive.

For consider:

(a) $[P \vee (Q \,\&\, \sim Q)] \supset P$.

The antecedent of (a) is contingent since a disjunction always gets the modal value of a "higher" disjunct; and P, so we may assume, is purely contingent. Hence, by the above definition,

$$[P \vee (Q \,\&\, \sim Q)] \overset{n}{\twoheadrightarrow} P.$$

But contraposition breaks down since $\sim [P \vee (Q \,\&\, \sim Q)]$ is truth-functionally equivalent to $[\sim P \,\&\, \sim (Q \,\&\, \sim Q)]$, and this is not purely contingent.[1]

6. It should be noticed, in passing, that Anderson and Belnap have to give up the idea that "P necessitates Q" in Smiley's sense, or "P necessitates Q" in my sense (i.e. in the sense of "$\overset{n}{\twoheadrightarrow}$"), is a sufficient condition for "P entails Q" *in their* sense of "entails". For obviously, if either condition *were* sufficient we could derive:

$[\sim P \,\&\, (P \vee Q)]$ entails Q.

7. It seems clear that my "strict entailment" is free of Lewis's paradoxes. Lewis's second proof breaks down at step (I).[2]

---

[1] Cf. D. Holdcroft's review of my 1958 paper, *Journal of Symbolic Logic*, vol. 25, Dec. 1960 (publ. October 1962). Holdcroft suggests in effect that (3') should be amended to "$\sim P'$ is purely contingent", an idea at which I had myself arrived a little earlier, although primarily in order to restore transitivity. This aspect of the matter Holdcroft does not discuss.   [2] See Chapter 9.

For:

$$P \twoheadrightarrow [(P \& Q) \lor (P \& \sim Q)]$$

is false: condition (2) of the definition of "$\twoheadrightarrow$" is not satisfied.

Lewis's first proof, on the other hand, breaks down at (δ), that is, at the step which corresponds to the law of disjunctive syllogism.

In other words,

  (α) $[\sim P \& (P \lor Q)] \twoheadrightarrow Q$

is false since it fails to satisfy condition (3) of the definition.

This can be proved as follows. Let us call the antecedent of the above, Δ. (That is, $\Delta = \sim P \& (P \lor Q)$.)

Now:

$$\begin{aligned}
\sim \Delta &\equiv \sim [\sim P \& (P \lor Q)] \\
&\equiv \sim \sim P \lor \sim (P \lor Q) \\
&\equiv P \lor \sim (P \lor Q) \\
&\equiv P \lor (\sim P \& \sim Q) \\
&\equiv (P \lor \sim P) \& (P \lor \sim Q).^{1}
\end{aligned}$$

Hence the negation of the antecedent of:

$$[\sim P \& (P \lor Q)] \supset Q$$

is *not* purely contingent. Hence (α) is false.

We may also notice that since $\sim \Delta \equiv [(P \lor \sim P) \& (P \lor \sim Q)]$, it follows that

$$\begin{aligned}
\Delta &\equiv \sim [(P \lor \sim P) \& (P \lor \sim Q)] \\
&\equiv \sim (P \lor \sim P) \lor \sim (P \lor \sim Q) \\
&\equiv \sim (P \lor \sim P) \lor (\sim P \& \sim \sim Q) \\
&\equiv \sim (P \lor \sim P) \lor (\sim P \& Q).
\end{aligned}$$

That is, the antecedent of :

$$[\sim P \& (P \lor Q)] \supset Q$$

is truth-functionally equivalent to a *disjunction* a disjunct of which is logically impossible.

8. I have already mentioned that it seems impossible to generalize my definition of strict entailment beyond the propositional calculus. Moreover, there is the following difficulty. On a pre-formal level one might say that the tautologousness of $P \supset Q$ may be grounded on, that is, follows from, each of the following *five* conditions:

  (*a*) *P* entails *Q*, in an intuitive sense which is to be analysed;

---

[1] The laws used in these transformations are of course: (1) $\sim (P \& Q) \equiv (\sim P \lor \sim Q)$, (2) $\sim \sim P \equiv P$, (3) $\sim (P \lor Q) \equiv (\sim P \& \sim Q)$, and (4) $[P \lor (Q \& R)] \equiv [(P \lor Q) \& (P \lor R)]$.

(*b*) Q is tautologous;

(*c*) ~ P is tautologous.

(*d*) There is a proposition R such that (α) Q is truth-functionally equivalent to R, (β) at least one conjunct of R is tautologous and (γ) P entails that conjunct of R which is not tautologous (or those conjuncts of R which are not tautologous, if there are several such conjuncts).

(*e*) There is a proposition R such that (α) P is truth-functionally equivalent to R, (β) R contains at least one disjunct the negation of which is tautologous, and (γ) Q is entailed by that disjunct of R the negation of which is not tautologous (or by those disjuncts of R the respective negations of which are not tautologous, if there are several such disjuncts).

Now it is clear, I think, that Smiley's necessitation is an attempt to exclude cases (*b*) and (*c*). My necessitation (i.e. strict necessitation), on the other hand, is an attempt to exclude (*d*) as well as (*b*) and (*c*). So each of these attempts tries to define entailment by putting a "sieve" on strict implication. Moreover, if my conjecture about Anderson and Belnap's system is right, that system is also an attempt to define entailment by putting a "sieve" on strict implication (although Anderson and Belnap did not see it, and even, I think, denied it). Their system is in fact an attempt to exclude (*e*) as well as (*b*), (*c*) and (*d*).[1] But, as we have already seen in effect, there is a radical difference between (*b*), (*c*) and (*d*) on the one hand, and (*e*) on the other hand. The first three cases can be excluded by forbidding suppression of necessarily true *premisses*. The last case can only be excluded by forbidding suppression of a *metalogical principle* (viz. the principle of bivalence).

But if so, then the exclusion of (*e*) is a fundamentally different matter from the exclusion of the other three cases. For in the latter cases one can say "Q does not follow from P taken by itself; another premiss (albeit a necessarily true one) has to be added to P". But in the case of (*e*) one *cannot* say this. For here Q does follow from *P taken by itself*. Of course, it only follows from P taken by itself if we grant the principle of bivalence. But if we do grant it, then Q *does follow* from *P taken by itself*. (It is, I think, for this reason that Lewis's first proof is intuitively much more compelling than

---

1 Whenever I talk here about excluding some or all of the conditions (*b*), (*c*), (*d*) and (*e*) I do so only for the sake of brevity, and mean excluding the implications which satisfy the conditions in question but do *not* satisfy the conditions (*a*).

his second proof.)[1] Thus we come to the conclusion that the intuitive idea expressed by "Q follows from P taken by itself" is even more obscure than it may at first seem to be.

The question now arises: How is one to elucidate it? We may be inclined to suppose that there are two ways of doing so. (1) By forbidding premiss suppression only; and (2) by forbidding principle suppression as well. Now the first way is at least *prima facie* plausible. For it is at least *prima facie* plausible to say "We must of course accept certain metalogical principles; but given these principles, we wish so to define entailment that in order that P should entail Q, Q must follow from P taken by itself". The trouble *here* is that when this is clarified and made more precise, it leads to non-transitivity (and non-contrapositivity too, if we wish to exclude (*d*) as well as (*b*) and (*c*)), and hence can't be regarded as a satisfactory reconstruction of the intuitive concept of entailment.

But the second way in which, it seems, one might elucidate the idea, is in a very different position. For in view of the fact that *some* principles have to be assumed to make inference possible at all, how do we tell which principles *may* be assumed and which may *not*? And *why* is the principle of bivalence one that may *not* be assumed? I see no answers to these questions. It seems to me that it is only in the special case of the propositional calculus that a truth-condition which has the effect of forbidding principle suppression can be given at all. For here one can express the antecedent of (δ), in Lewis's first proof, as a disjunction containing an anti-tautologous disjunct.

If this is right, then the most one can say for the Anderson and Belnap system is that this is what one gets when one constructs a theory of entailment based on a logic which does not assume the principle of bivalence. If one restricts oneself to the propositional calculus, Anderson and Belnap have shown in effect, then one can formalize the very vague intuitive idea of "Q follows from P with the help of as few assumptions "outside" P as possible". (Here "assumptions" includes principles as well as premisses.) And, they have shown, one will then get a relation of logical implication which is transitive, reflexive and adjunctive, holds in the class of all

---

[1] Also, I believe it is for this reason that some philosophers have been inclined to think that Lewis's *second* proof went wrong in asserting that P entails [(P & Q) ∨ (P & ∼ Q)], but that his *first* proof went wrong in asserting that (P & Q) entails P – they thought they *must* accept that [∼ P & (P ∨ Q)] entails Q.

propositions (in the propositional calculus), and yet is "paradox free". But the relation is not really acceptable, even for the propositional calculus, as a reconstruction of our inconsistent preformal concept of entailment, although it is, of course, a *possible* reconstruction. And this is so because the rejection of the principle of bivalence seems too high a price to pay for avoiding Lewis's paradoxes. In my opinion, nearly all of our ordinary thought clearly presupposes the principle of bivalence. In some areas we have vague intuitions which seem to conflict with it; but it is entirely unclear whether the rejection of the principle is really coherent.

In any case, there seems to be no way of constructing a theory of entailment on the Anderson–Belnap lines for at least a large class of cases falling outside the propositional calculus. And, if so, then the idea of Q following from P on minimal additional assumptions, seems to be of little use in the analysis of entailment.

9. I wish now to return briefly to my definition of "strict entailment". As I said earlier, I see no way of so generalizing the definition as to cover all the cases that do not fall within the propositional calculus.

At first one might think that this could be done as follows.

$P \twoheadrightarrow Q$ if and only if $P \supset Q$ is a substitution instance of $P' \supset Q'$ such that

(1) $P' \supset Q'$ is logically necessary,

(2) Q' is purely contingent,

(3) $\sim P'$ is purely contingent.

Paradox 4, however, shows that this relation will *not* be transitive. For here the first two steps will be all right, but "There are exactly ten brothers" will not strictly entail "There are exactly as many brothers as brothers", since the corresponding material implication is not a substitution instance of any implication which satisfies (1), (2) and (3). Thus the derivation of the "paradoxical" conclusion breaks down at the transitivity step.

Hence, the new relation won't be transitive and therefore won't be an acceptable reconstruction of entailment.

10. Perhaps my definition of "$\twoheadrightarrow$" can be generalized in such a way as not to lead to the loss of transitivity. But I cannot see any such way. It may be suggested, however, that the conjecture which I made in § 1 is wrong, namely the conjecture that in the calculus of propositions strict entailment is unrestrictedly transitive. (And

if this conjecture is wrong, then my conjecture in § 2 is also wrong.)
I do not think that this is the case, but I cannot of course be certain.
In the calculus of propositions my definition enables us to break
Lewis's first proof at (δ), and his second proof at (I). Hence, these
steps are simply invalid and we do not therefore have a valid proof
of Q in the first case or of $(Q \vee \sim Q)$ in the second case. But with
a language as rich as that of Paradox *4*, there is no step in the proof,
other than the final step involving transitivity, which could with
the *slightest* plausibility be considered invalid: any adequate theory
of entailment would have to accept those other steps as valid. So
far as I can see, this doesn't prove my conjecture of § 1: it is possible that my definition breaks Lewis's proofs *both* at the respective
steps mentioned above *and* at the final step. But I see no reason to
think so.

11. Let us now return to the alternative of restricting entailment
to *contingent* propositions. As I explained earlier, this is strongly
counter-intuitive, and it would also make it impossible for us to
have any *general* theory of entailment.

In any case, however, the attempt would not be free of difficulty.
Suppose we say:

> P entails Q if and only if
>
> (1) $P \supset Q$ is logically necessary,
> (2) Q is purely contingent,
> (3) $\sim P$ is purely contingent.

We shall then have to reject the principle that $(P \,\&\, Q)$ entails P,
and also the principle that $[\sim P \,\&\, (P \vee Q)]$ entails Q.

Suppose we say:

> P entails Q if and only if
>
> (1) $P \supset Q$ is logically necessary,
> (2) Q is purely contingent,
> (3) P is contingent.

We shall then have to reject the principle that $(P \,\&\, Q)$ entails P,
and we shall also have to give up contraposition.

Suppose we say:

> P entails Q if and only if
>
> (1) $P \supset Q$ is logically necessary,
> (2) Q is contingent,
> (3) P is contingent.

We shall then have to reject the principle that $(P \,\&\, Q)$ entails P, and in addition we shall have the old trouble that P will entail $[P \mathbin{\&} (Q \vee \sim Q)]$.

All this shows that the attempt to restrict entailment to contingent propositions, apart from its *basic* counter-intuitiveness which I have already explained, would be a tricky undertaking and would involve additional counter-intuitive consequences. Yet Wisdom, Strawson and others seemed to think that this course was entirely simple and that it was an obvious solution of the problem.

INDEX OF PROPER NAMES